Indian Cooking for Family and Friends

MEENA PATHAK
INDIAN COOKING
FOR **FAMILY** AND **FRIENDS**

NEW HOLLAND

I dedicate this book to my three children, Neeraj, Nayan, and Anjali, who all share the same passion for food and love of spice as their mother.

First published in 2004 by New Holland Publishers (UK) Ltd

Garfield House, 86-88 Edgware Road, London W2 2EA, UK
www.newhollandpublishers.com

Library of Congress Cataloging-in-Publication Data Available

ISBN 1 84330 825 8

Senior Editor: Clare Sayer
American Editor: Beverly LeBlanc
Patak's Development Chef: Sunil Menon
Design: Roger Hammond
Photographer: John Freeman
Assistant photographer: Alex Dow
Stylist: Labeena Ishaque
Production: Hazel Kirkman
Editorial Direction: Rosemary Wilkinson

10 9 8 7 6 5 4 3 2 1

Reproduction by Pica Digital PTE Ltd, Singapore
Printed and bound by Times Offset (M) Sdn. Bhd., Malaysia

NOTES
· All eggs are extra-large unless otherwise stated

CONTENTS

INTRODUCTION

The inspiration for this, my second cookbook, is really all about showing people how to cook good Indian food for themselves on an everyday basis. It is a recipe collection that reflects my life and how I like to cook and eat—I really wanted to prove you do not have to attempt the whole Indian restaurant banquet experience in your home every time you want to cook Indian food. I lead a full and often very hectic life, however, I believe there should always be time for good delicious food—whether I am preparing a quick evening meal for myself and my husband, Kirit, made with whatever ingredients I have in the refrigerator, a casual lunch for a friend or a dinner for a big family celebration. The demands of a busy lifestyle mean I have had to adapt some classic Indian dishes to make them easier to prepare, however, I will never compromise on flavor. I personally do not enjoy bland food and want to show people that with a little bit of spice it is easy to produce the most mouthwatering dishes. It is important, though, not to confuse spice with heat—of course, some of my recipes do have a chili "kick" but what they have more than anything are delicious complex flavors that come from the spices I use. To me this is what real Indian food is all about.

Most of us (myself included) simply don't have the time to spend long hours in the kitchen and we also want to use ingredients that are readily available in grocery stores. "You are what you eat" is a statement that I strongly believe in, so food should also be as naturally healthy as possible with an eye kept on the fat content. My love of spices is always at the heart of my cooking and I love experimenting with different flavors, using influences from other cuisines as well as from India.

All the ideas for the recipes have come from personal experience—the food I ate as a child in India, what I saw and experienced on my many travels, and, of course, my family's favorite dishes. I sincerely hope you will enjoy cooking these dishes and will maybe also be inspired to create some of your own.

How we eat today

The way we cook and eat today has changed dramatically since I first came to live in England. As a child growing up in India, I watched and learned how our food was prepared—ingredients were available only in season and everything was done as part of a ritual, from grinding whole spices to making fresh paneer cheese to filling endless triangles of pastry to make deliciously spicy samosas. I still insist on grinding my own spices, but I recognize that, with more demands on our time, we want to spend less time in the kitchen and more time enjoying the food that we are preparing. Ten or so years ago, many of the ingredients that are essential to Indian cooking were difficult to find, but now most of them are readily available in good supermarkets or Asian groceries. All of this is good news for Indian cooking.

One other change is that people's tastes have become much more sophisticated—eating out is no longer reserved just for special occasions and as more and more people indulge in foreign holidays, they become more willing to experience different cultures and to try new flavors.

When my children were growing up we always ate together as a family at the end of the day, and I still believe in the importance of family meals. However, there are times when you just need a quick snack or a simple bite to eat and so I have included some of my favorite "quick fix" dishes in this collection.

Menu planning

Traditionally Indians eat three meals a day, but breakfast and lunch are often combined and snacking is practically second nature to Indians. A full Indian meal usually consists of a "wet" dish or "curry," which can be meat, fish or paneer or legumes for vegetarians, one or two vegetable dishes, yogurt or raita, rice or breads and, of course, pickles. When planning a meal it is essential to create a balance and to have a combination of flavors and textures that complement each other. Color is also vital—I always try to serve a green vegetable dish with meat and fish dishes. Many of the recipes in this book work particularly well with certain accompaniments and I have suggested these where relevant, but don't be afraid to experiment with your own combinations.

Catering for large numbers

One of the most important things to remember when you are entertaining or cooking for large numbers is to make it easy on yourself. Cooking should be fun, so if you are not an experienced cook, don't worry! Don't try to do something that is too complicated and choose some dishes that can be prepared ahead. A great way to cater for a large party is to let your guests help themselves—buffet food and snack dishes such as pop-padums will keep guests happy and can look very impressive presented on large plates with simple garnishes and lots of pickles.

Preparing in advance

One of the things I have tried to do in this book is to make the recipes as easy to cook as possible. Many people still think that preparing and cooking Indian food requires a lot of preparation, but with a few time-saving tricks you will soon realize that cooking good, healthy Indian food is something that can be done at any time, for any occasion.

As you look through the recipes in this book you will see that some ingredients appear often and form the basis for many dishes. Garlic, ginger, and onions are used extensively in Indian cooking. Buying and preparing these from scratch every time you want to cook an Indian dish can be time-consuming and laborious, so here are my ideas and tips to help you on your way.

Garlic

A large number of Indian recipes call for garlic pulp. One large clove will make about ½ teaspoon of garlic pulp. You can prepare it in batches and keep it for later. Simply peel the garlic cloves and puree in a food processor or blender with a little water until you have a smooth pulp. This will keep in airtight containers in the refrigerator for up to ten days. You can also freeze garlic pulp in ice-cube trays kept specifically for this purpose. Once frozen, remove from the trays and store in the freezer in airtight containers.

Fresh ginger

Ginger pulp is also a basic ingredient in many of my recipes. Simply peel the outer skin with a sharp knife and roughly chop the ginger into small pieces. Puree in a food processor or blender with a little water until you have a smooth consistency. Again, you can store this in the refrigerator in airtight containers or freeze as above. I usually leave my ginger unpeeled because there is a lot of flavor in the skin.

Onions

Onions are used in Indian cooking in many different ways—to flavor, color, thicken, or garnish dishes. If onions are being used to make a rich sauce for a meat dish they are usually fried slowly in oil or ghee. You can fry batches of sliced onions in advance and keep them in the refrigerator in airtight containers for up to two weeks.

Using herbs and spices

Herbs

The most commonly used fresh herb in Indian cooking is cilantro and there really is no substitute. Fresh cilantro can quickly lose its flavor but you can freeze it by washing the leaves well, leaving them to dry on a towel, and then freezing in sealed plastic bags. It can then be used in cooking, although not as a garnish. Other fresh herbs such as fenugreek leaves and curry leaves can also be stored in this way. Fried curry leaves are used as a garnish in dishes from southern India. You can prepare these in advance: simply fry in hot oil for 2–3 minutes, then remove them from the pan with a slotted spoon, drain on paper towels and, when cool, store in an airtight container for up to ten days.

Spices

Spices are an important part of Indian culture—and not just because they are used extensively in the cooking. Many of the spices that we use today have been part of Ayurvedic medicine for thousands of years. Once you have discovered how spices work and what the most common flavor combinations are, you will soon be able to experiment and flavor your dishes to your own liking. (See pages 122–123 for more information.)

In Indian cooking there are spices that are always used at the beginning of a recipe, such as mustard seeds and cumin seeds. They are usually added to hot oil and when they start to crackle you add your "wet" ingredients, such as garlic, ginger, and onions. Ground spices are added after you have added the vegetables—they need to go in last otherwise they will burn and change the color and flavor of the dish. Garam masala is usually always added right at the end of a recipe—it only needs to be cooked for a few minutes, but enhances the flavor of a finished dish.

Spices really stay fresh for only about four weeks. Ground spices deteriorate even more quickly than whole ones because their essential oils evaporate more quickly. It is always best to buy whole spices and then dry-roast and grind them, as and when you need them. The best way to store them is in airtight tins in a cupboard away from direct sunlight. Because I cook for my family every day, I grind up my spices in small quantities on a regular basis. Buy small quantities at a time and leave them quite coarsely ground—the finer they're ground the more quickly they lose their flavor.

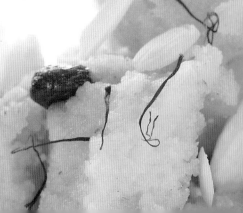

Basic recipes

GARAM MASALA

There are countless different ways of preparing garam masala, and in India every household probably has its own special recipe, handed down through the generations. The basic mixture also varies throughout the regions of India. The mixture usually includes the spices cardamom, cloves, cinnamon, and nutmeg. Here is my recipe for garam masala. This quantity lasts me for a few weeks—you might prefer to make less if you are not cooking Indian food on a daily basis.

5 ounces cumin seeds

2½ ounces coriander seeds

2 ounces green cardamom pods

1½ ounces black cardamom pods

20 x 1-inch pieces of cinnamon stick

¾ ounce cloves

4 ounces fennel seeds

½ ounce bay leaves

2 whole nutmegs

Dry-roast all the spices by putting them in a preheated cast-iron skillet. Stir over medium heat for 3 minutes, or until the mixture starts smoking slightly. Remove from the heat and leave to cool on paper towels. Transfer to a coffee or spice grinder and process until you have a fine powder (although I prefer to leave my mixture quite coarse). Store in a dry, airtight container with a tight-fitting lid and keep out of direct sunlight. Use within one month.

CHAPATTI

Chapattis are eaten all over India as an accompaniment to most meals—they really are a national bread. The art is in the shaping—a good chapatti should be perfectly round and flat.

makes ten

1⅔ cups wholewheat flour, sifted

½ teaspoon salt (optional)

1 tablespoon vegetable oil

melted ghee or butter

Mix the flour, salt and ⅔ cup water in a bowl. Add the oil and knead to a soft dough. Leave covered with a wet cloth for 30 minutes.

Knead the dough again on a floured countertop for about 10 minutes, then divide into 10 pieces using a little flour to shape them into round balls. Press out each piece on a floured board using your fingers. Roll out with a rolling pin into thin pancakes about 4–5 inches in diameter.

Heat a flat griddle or a skillet. Cook each chapatti over a medium heat for 30 seconds and when one side dries up and tiny bubbles begin to appear, turn it over and cook until brown spots appear on the under surface. Press the sides down gently with a clean dish towel.

Remove the chapatti from the griddle with a pair of tongs and place directly over the heat/flame until it puffs up. Smear one side with a little ghee or butter and serve immediately.

PARATHA

Parathas originated in the north of India, where wheat is a staple.

makes six

1⅔ cups wholewheat flour, sifted

½ teaspoon salt

1 tablespoon vegetable oil

6 tablespoons ghee or butter, melted

extra flour for dusting

Put the flour, salt, and ⅔ cup water in a bowl and knead to a soft dough. Mix in the oil and set aside, covered, for 30 minutes.

Divide the dough into 6 equal parts and shape into round balls. Flatten and roll out into flat disks about 5 inches in diameter.

Smear a little ghee onto the top of the paratha, then fold it over into a semicircle. Smear more ghee over the upper surface and fold it again to form a triangle shape. Place it on a floured board and roll into a thin triangle, making sure the edges are not thick.

Place on a hot griddle. Cook for 1 minute, then turn over. When the paratha begins to color, brush a little ghee on one side, turn over and cook again. Brush a little ghee on this side also.

Cook for a few more seconds until the paratha is golden brown on both sides.

PERFECT BASMATI RICE

Rice is one of the main staples of Indian food, particularly in the south, where you are likely to eat rice at every meal. I always recommend using basmati rice as its aromatic flavor is far superior

to other varieties. Cooking perfect rice is really very simple.

serves four

2 cups basmati rice

4 cups hot water

Wash the basmati rice in several changes of warm water and then set aside for 20 minutes in a colander. Place the rice in a large pan and cover with 4 cups of water. Bring to a boil, stir gently, and then cover. Leave to simmer for 10 minutes until all the water has been absorbed.

CUMIN RICE

This is a wonderfully simple rice dish that will be eaten every day in most Indian households—it is also very simple to make. I certainly prefer it to plain rice. The cumin seeds complement the fragrant basmati rice perfectly.

serves four

1¼ cups basmati rice

1½ tablespoons vegetable oil

2 cloves

2 cardamom pods

1 bay leaf

1 teaspoon cumin seeds

½ teaspoon salt

Wash the rice in several changes of water and then leave to soak in a large bowl of cold water.

In a karhai, wok, or large pan

Left: **Perfect basmati rice**

heat the oil and add the cloves, cardamom pods, bay leaf, and cumin seeds. When the cumin seeds begin to crackle, drain the rice and add it to the pan.

Fry over low heat until the oil coats the rice grains.

Add the salt and pour in 2½ cups hot water and stir lightly to make sure the rice does not stick to the bottom of the pan. Bring to a boil, then reduce the heat and simmer, covered, for 10 minutes until the water is absorbed and the rice is cooked.

If the rice is cooked and the water is not completely absorbed, remove the lid to let the water evaporate. Remove the cardamom pods before serving.

CILANTRO AND MINT RAITA

This lovely bright green raita is delicious as a dip for poppadums, koftas, or other fried snacks. It is also wonderful with kabobs. In an Indian household it will be made fresh every day, but you can keep it for up to a week in the refrigerator.

serves four

5 ounces fresh cilantro

2 ounces fresh mint

1 green chili, chopped

4 cloves garlic, crushed

juice of ½ lime

1 cup thick natural yogurt

½ teaspoon sugar

salt, to taste

Place the fresh cilantro, fresh mint, green chili, and garlic in a food processor or blender and process to a fine paste. Add the lime juice and a little water, if required.

Place the yogurt in a bowl and whisk in the green paste. Stir in the sugar and salt.

You can prepare this ahead by freezing the green paste without the yogurt.

MIXED VEGETABLE RAITA

This fresh tasting raita is a classic accompaniment to biryani dishes.

serves four

1¼ cups natural yogurt

1½ teaspoons sugar

salt, to taste

1 teaspoon cumin seeds, roasted and ground (see page 22)

½ cup chopped onions

½ cup finely diced tomatoes

½ cup seeded and chopped cucumber

1 tablespoon chopped fresh cilantro

Mix the yogurt and sugar together with a whisk. Stir in salt and the ground roasted cumin.

Add the onions, tomatoes, and cucumber, and serve garnished with chopped cilantro.

DATE AND LIME CHUTNEY

One of my favorite relishes to serve with a hot meal, this also tastes equally good as a sandwich spread. It is unlike a fresh relish because it takes about 2 weeks to mature. Once opened, it will keep for 2-3 months in the refrigerator.

makes about 4 pounds

10–12 limes, each cut into 4 wedges

3 tablespoons sea salt

20 dried red chilies

1 tablespoon black mustard seeds

1¼ cups white vinegar

15 cloves garlic, peeled

1½ tablespoons ginger pulp

1¾ cups sugar

14 ounces pitted dates

⅓ cup golden raisins

2 ounces crystallized ginger, chopped

2 ounces candied peel, chopped

The first step is to rub the lime wedges with the sea salt and place them in a glass or ceramic jar with a nonmetallic lid. Seal the jar and leave the limes to mature at room temperature, or in the sun, for 2 weeks.

After 2 weeks continue with the recipe. Place the red chilies and mustard seeds in the vinegar and leave to infuse for 4–6 hours. Grind the vinegar and spices to a paste in a blender with the garlic cloves and ginger pulp.

Heat a cast-iron (not aluminum) pan and add the blended paste together with the sugar. Bring to a boil, then add the dates, golden raisins, crystallized ginger, candied peel and salted limes. Bring the mixture to a simmer, stirring constantly. Cook for 15 minutes, turn off the heat. Put the chutney into sterilized jars while still hot and leave to cool.

Place a circle of waxed paper, waxed side down, over the chutney. Seal the jars and store in a cool place. Once opened, keep in the refrigerator.

Tip Sterilize jam jars and their lids (plastic-coated lids are necessary because the vinegar in chutney can corrode metal) by washing them in warm, soapy water. Rinse thoroughly in warm water and dry well with a dish towel. Stand them on a baking tray and place in a warm oven for 10 minutes—this also prevents them from cracking when filling them with the hot chutney.

SPICED PINEAPPLE RELISH

This spicy sweet-and-sour combination is fairly common in India, served as an accompaniment with spicy dishes.

serves four

1 medium fresh pineapple, diced

1 small onion, finely diced (optional)

1 teaspoon salt

1 teaspoon ground cumin

1 teaspoon garam masala

1 green chili, finely diced

1 teaspoon sugar

1 teaspoon chopped mint leaves

Combine all the ingredients in a bowl. The onion is optional, but I like to include it as it adds a bit of crunch. Toss gently with a wooden spoon, then serve at room temperature.

SPICED GRAVY

Gravy recipes are not that common in India because so many dishes are prepared with their own delicious sauce. For my children, however, I have included this recipe which uses bouillon cubes. Serve the gravy hot with roast meats and mashed potatoes.

serves four

1 tablespoon vegetable oil

1 inch piece cinnamon stick

4 cloves

2 bay leaves

1 onion, diced

1–2 chicken or beef bouillon cubes

2¼ cups warm water

1 tablespoon all-purpose flour

½ can (14-oz) canned crushed tomatoes

2 tablespoons mango or chili pickle

Heat the oil in a skillet. Add the cinnamon stick, cloves, and bay leaves and stir briefly. Add the diced onion and cook until translucent. Meanwhile, stir the bouillon cubes with the warm water in a mixing bowl or jug.

Add the flour to the onion mixture and stir constantly for 2-3 minutes, making sure it does not become lumpy. Add the canned chopped tomatoes and cook for 1 minute longer before adding the bouillon mixture. Keep stirring to avoid sticking and lumps. When the gravy starts to thicken, stir in the mango or chili pickle, then serve.

LASSI

Drinking lassi is a great way to beat the heat of the scorching sun in summer. Yogurt has many health-giving properties and this drink is perfect for settling the stomach—particularly after a very spicy Indian meal. It can be served sweet or salted.

serves four

1¾ cups natural yogurt

5 tablespoons sugar or 1½ teaspoons salt

1 teaspoon roasted coriander seeds, crushed

pistachio slivers, to garnish

Pour the yogurt into a bowl, add the sugar or salt and slightly less than 1 cup chilled water. Whisk well until all the sugar or salt has dissolved and all the lumps of yogurt are broken down, leaving a smooth flowing liquid. Stir in the coriander seeds and serve chilled, garnished with pistachio slivers.

ICED LIME WATER

This refreshing drink is served all over India during the summer. It is often served as a welcome drink.

serves four

5 tablespoons sugar

juice of 1 lime

½ teaspoon salt

fresh mint and lemon slices, to garnish

Mix 3 cups water and the sugar together in a bowl until the sugar dissolves. Add the lime juice and salt and stir well. Serve with ice, fresh mint leaves, and lemon slices.

Tip Squeezing fresh limes can be hard work. I put mine in the microwave for 10 seconds before squeezing them—this makes it much easier.

quick fixes

There are times when putting together a full Indian meal simply isn't possible and there are plenty of days when all I want is a fast bite to eat. This chapter is all about fast and delicious ways to eat when time is short—perhaps when a friend has dropped by for lunch or when you just feel like a tasty snack to keep you going. The spicy French toast is a great breakfast or brunch dish and takes just minutes to prepare, while my Bombay mixed vegetable sandwich is an intriguing take on a classic snack.

EGGPLANT DIP

1½ pounds eggplants

2 cloves garlic, finely chopped

1 tablespoon finely chopped fresh
    cilantro

1–2 finely chopped fresh green chilies

1 tomato, finely chopped

¾ teaspoon salt

1 small onion, finely chopped

1 tablespoon finely chopped chives

1 teaspoon ground cumin

2 teaspoons lemon juice or natural yogurt

1 tablespoon vegetable oil

1 teaspoon garam masala

½ teaspoon sugar

hot naan bread, toast, poppadums, or
    crackers, to serve

Eggplants are a wonderfully versatile vegetable—this dip is a particular favorite with my family and friends. It is great with poppadums, but any kind of crispy snack will do.

Place the whole eggplants under a heated broiler and broil for 15–20 minutes until the skin is black and burned on all sides and the flesh is soft and "pulp". Remove it from the broiler and leave to cool to room temperature, before peeling off all the skin and removing the stems. Place the eggplant flesh in a bowl and mash farther, using a potato masher or a wooden spoon.

Add all the remaining ingredients to the eggplant puree and stir well. Serve cold with hot naan bread, toast, poppadums, or crackers.

Tip To cook the eggplants without having to watch them, wrap them in foil, put them on a baking tray and bake in a heated oven, 350°F, for 20–25 minutes.

SPICY FRENCH TOAST

3 eggs

1 tablespoon milk

pinch of salt

½ teaspoon ground turmeric

½ teaspoon ground cumin

1 green chili, finely chopped

1 teaspoon chopped fresh cilantro

1 tablespoon butter, melted

1 onion, finely diced

1 tablespoon oil

4 slices of bread, crusts removed

This recipe originally started off as a spicy omelet until I decided to dip bread in the mixture.

Break the eggs into a bowl and add the milk, salt, ground turmeric, ground cumin, chili, fresh cilantro, melted butter, and onion; whisk well.

Heat the oil in a pan. Dip each slice of bread, one at a time, into the egg mixture, making sure the egg coats the bread evenly. Transfer the bread slices to the pan and cook for about 3 minutes over medium heat until light brown. Turn the bread over and cook the other side for the same length of time. Serve hot.

Opposite: **Spicy French toast**

SPICED GROUND LAMB BALLS

serves four

1¼ pounds ground lamb or beef

1 egg

2 onions, finely chopped

1 tablespoon finely chopped fresh
   cilantro, plus extra to garnish

½ teaspoon ground turmeric

1 teaspoon cayenne pepper

1 teaspoon garam masala

½ teaspoon garlic pulp

1 teaspoon ginger pulp

pinch of ground nutmeg (optional)

½ teaspoon salt

vegetable oil, for shallow frying

Cilantro and Mint Raita, to serve

These are usually served as a snack with Cilantro and Mint Raita (see page 13), however, I always make double the quantity and freeze half so I can enjoy them another time.

Combine all the ingredients, except the oil, in a bowl, mixing well, to make a fairly sticky mixture; divide into 20–25 balls.

Heat the vegetable oil in a shallow skillet. Cook 6 meatballs at a time, immersing them in the oil and gently swirling the oil around, to brown them on all sides, for 3–4 minutes; drain on paper towels.

Sprinkle with cilantro and serve hot or cold with Cilantro and Mint Raita.

PASTA WITH **CURRY** SAUCE

1 tablespoon butter

½ teaspoon cumin seeds

1 large onion, sliced

1 teaspoon garlic pulp

½ teaspoon ground turmeric

1 teaspoon garam masala

1 green bell pepper, seeded and sliced

1 red bell pepper, seeded and sliced

3 tablespoons light cream

salt

11 ounces cooked pasta

1 cup grated cheese, to serve

My children love this recipe. They used to eat only plain pasta until they saw me changing the flavor of leftover pasta and now they will not have it any other way! Grated sharp cheddar tastes better than Parmesan cheese as a topping.

Melt the butter in a pan and add the cumin seeds. When they begin to crackle, add the sliced onions and fry for 5–8 minutes. Add the garlic pulp, ground turmeric, and garam masala and continue to fry over low heat.

Add the green and red bell peppers and cook for 3–5 minutes longer. Stir in the cream and salt to taste.

Add the cooked pasta to the sauce, sprinkle with grated cheese, and serve hot.

SPICED BEANS
ON NAAN BREAD

serves two

1 teaspoon vegetable oil

1 teaspoon cumin seeds

1 green chili, seeded and chopped

pinch of asafoetida

1 can (14-oz) baked beans

2 mini naan breads

1 tablespoon grated cheddar cheese,

1 teaspoon chopped fresh cilantro

1 tablespoon chopped onion

This very simple dish is quick to make and is an all-time favorite with my husband.

Heat the oil, then add the cumin seeds. When they begin to crackle, add the green chili and asafoetida. After 30 seconds add the baked beans and give the mixture a good stir, then reduce the heat.

Place the naan breads on a cookie sheet. When the beans are heated through, tip them onto each naan bread. Sprinkle the grated cheese, cilantro, and onions over the beans.

Place under a heated broiler and broil briefly until the cheese melts and becomes golden brown. Serve at once and eat hot.

MASALA POPPADUMS

1 onion, chopped

2 potatoes, peeled, boiled, and chopped

1 large tomato, chopped

2 tablespoons chopped fresh cilantro

1–2 green chilies, chopped and seeded or

½ teaspoon cayenne pepper

¼ teaspoon salt

1 teaspoon cracked black pepper

1 teaspoon roasted cumin seeds, crushed

(see Tip)

1 tablespoon lemon juice

4 cooked poppadums

Poppadums are an extremely popular snack throughout India, as well as in the many Indian restaurants outside India. My family loves this fun way of eating them, which they like to call "Go Crackers!"

Mix all the ingredients, except the poppadums, together in a bowl and divide into 4 portions. Sprinkle a portion over each poppadum and serve immediately so they don't become soggy.

Tip To roast cumin seeds, place them in a glass bowl or on a plate and cook in the microwave on High for 30–40 seconds. Crush coarsely using a mortar and pestle. Roasted cumin can be stored in an airtight container at room temperature for 2–3 months.

CHEESE-STUFFED PEPPERS

serves two to four

1 cup grated cheddar cheese

1 onion, diced

1 tomato, chopped

1 fresh green or red chili, chopped

½ teaspoon ground black pepper

1 tablespoon chopped fresh cilantro or

fresh basil

½ teaspoon Italian seasoning

1 teaspoon vegetable or olive oil

2 large red or green bell peppers, halved

lengthwise and seeded

Serve these peppers as an accompaniment to vegetarian or nonvegetarian main dishes, or as a snack with a green salad. An alternative, equally good version of the recipe below is to use 1⅔ cups of leftover mashed potato instead of cheese to fill the peppers, finishing off with a topping of grated cheese.

Heat the oven to 350°F.

Place all the ingredients, except the oil and the peppers, in a bowl and mix well.

Rub the oil over the skin of the pepper halves and stuff them equally with the cheese mixture. Arrange on a cookie sheet, place in the heated oven, and cook for 20 minutes. Serve at once.

Opposite: **Masala poppadums**

BOMBAY MIXED VEGETABLE SANDWICH

serves two

FOR THE SANDWICH

4 slices of good white bread

1 tablespoon butter

1 potato, boiled, peeled, and sliced into
    circles

2 tomatoes, sliced

1 small onion, sliced into rings

10 slices of cucumber

salt and pepper, to taste

FOR THE CILANTRO CHUTNEY

3 cups chopped fresh cilantro

2 tablespoons chopped mint leaves

3 cloves garlic, peeled

1-inch piece fresh ginger root,
    unpeeled and washed

¼ teaspoon salt

1 teaspoon sugar

2 green chilies

2 tablespoons lemon juice

This recipe brings back fond memories of my school days in Mumbai. I could never wait for the 11 o'clock break when we used to buy these sandwiches from the hawker stall outside the school gates! It is a great snack to take on picnics and is ideal served with hot soup. Once made, the Cilantro Chutney can be kept in the refrigerator for up to 10 days.

To make the Cilantro Chutney, place all the ingredients in a blender. Blend to a smooth paste, adding a little water if necessary to ease the blending. The resulting chutney will be fairly thick.

Spread the 4 slices of bread with the butter, then spread each slice with 1 tablespoon Cilantro Chutney. Lay 2 slices of the bread, chutney side up, on the countertop. Top with sliced potato, tomatoes, onion, and cucumber, sprinkling salt and pepper between each layer. Top with the remaining slices of bread. Cut diagonally and serve.

SPICED FRIED FISH

serves two

½ teaspoon ginger pulp

½ teaspoon garlic pulp

¼ teaspoon cayenne pepper

¼ teaspoon salt

½ teaspoon ground turmeric

1 tablespoon lemon juice

2 x 6 ounce flounder fillets

vegetable oil, for shallow frying

1 tablespoon rice flour

1 tablespoon semolina

I first had this dish, kurmuri tali macchi, at my aunt's weekend resort in Goa and have never forgotten it. It makes a great snack or appetizer served with some fresh raita (see page 14).

Mix the ginger, garlic, cayenne, salt, and ground turmeric with the lemon juice. Rub the mixture all over the fish fillets and leave for 5 minutes.

Heat the oil in a skillet. Mix together the rice flour and semolina, then dust or pat the fish with this mixture, pressing it onto the fish so it sticks well. Shallow fry the flounder for 2–3 minutes, then serve.

CHICKEN
WITH GREEN BELL PEPPERS

serves four

3 teaspoons garlic pulp

2 teaspoons garam masala

3 tablespoons vegetable oil

salt

4 boneless and skinless chicken breast
   halves, each cut into 3 strips

2 cloves

2 green cardamom pods

2 bay leaves

1 teaspoon cumin seeds

2 small onions, sliced

1 teaspoon ginger pulp

1 teaspoon ground turmeric

1 teaspoon cayenne pepper

3 teaspoons ground coriander

½ can (14-oz.) tomatoes, crushed

⅔ cup green pepper strips

3½ cup light cream, plus extra to garnish

1 teaspoon sugar

1 tablespoon chopped fresh cilantro, plus
   extra to garnish

When I was growing up in India, green bell peppers were avail-able only during the months of November, December, and January. During that time we certainly had our fill of this dish, known as murgh simla mirch—now I can prepare it all year.

Place the garlic pulp, half of the garam masala, 1 tablespoon of the oil, and 1 teaspoon of salt in a bowl and mix well. Add the chicken pieces and leave to marinate for about 2 hours.

Heat the remaining oil in a pan and add the cloves, cardamom pods, bay leaves, and cumin seeds. When they begin to crackle, add the sliced onions and fry for 10–15 minutes.

Add the ginger pulp and the ground spices (except the remaining garam masala). Fry over medium heat for 1 minute. Add the tomatoes and continue to cook over medium heat for 10 minutes. Add the green bell peppers and the cream. Add salt to taste, then add the sugar and remaining garam masala. Cook for 2–3 minutes, then add the chopped cilantro.

Cook the marinated chicken in a hot skillet or under a heated broiler for 5–8 minutes each side. Arrange in a serving dish and pour the tomato-and-green-pepper-sauce over the top. Serve garnished with cream and plenty of chopped fresh cilantro.

OKRA WITH ONIONS

2 tablespoons vegetable oil, plus extra for
   deep-frying

3½ cups diced okra

1 teaspoon cumin seeds

1-inch piece fresh ginger root, chopped

4 cloves garlic, chopped

1 green chili, chopped

½ teaspoon ground turmeric

2 medium onions, sliced

1 tomato, diced

1 teaspoon ground cumin

juice of ½ lemon

salt

1 tablespoon chopped fresh cilantro

This very simple dish, known in India as bhendi do pyaaza, has become an all-time favorite in Indian restaurants.

Heat the oil for deep-frying in a large heavy-bottomed pan to 350°F. Add the diced okra and deep-fry for 5–8 minutes until it becomes limp; drain and set aside.

Heat the 2 tablespoons oil in another pan and add the cumin seeds. When they begin to crackle, add the chopped ginger, chopped garlic, green chili, and ground turmeric. After 1 minute, add the sliced onions and fry over medium heat, stirring constantly, adding a little water to prevent sticking. Stir in the diced tomato.

When the onions have become soft, but not colored, add the deep-fried okra and stir well. Sprinkle with ground cumin, add the lemon juice, and season with salt to taste. Finally, add the chopped cilantro and serve hot.

GINGERY TURNIPS

serves four

1 tablespoon vegetable oil

1 teaspoon cumin seeds

pinch of asafoetida (optional)

1 teaspoon sesame seeds

2 green chilies, seeded and sliced

2-inch piece of fresh ginger root, peeled
   and cut into juliennes

3 cups peeled turnips cut into wedges

1 teaspoon salt

½ teaspoon sugar

1 tablespoon lemon juice

pinch of ground nutmeg

Eaten very often in the northern state of Kashmir, this recipe can also be made with Savoy cabbage, raw beet, radish, or zucchini instead of turnips. It can be eaten on its own, hot or cold, and it also works well as an accompaniment. It goes well with Smoked Lamb with Saffron (see page 112).

Heat the oil in a wok, karhai, or large pan, then add the cumin seeds and asafoetida, if using. When the cumin seeds start to crackle, add the sesame seeds. When they begin to brown, add the green chilies, ginger, and turnips. Cover and cook over low heat for 15 minutes, stirring occasionally.

Add the salt, sugar, and lemon juice. Cook for 2–3 minutes longer. Turn off the heat and sprinkle with nutmeg. Serve the turnips hot or cold.

Opposite: **Okra with onions**

SPICY SPINACH WITH EGGS

serves four

2 tablespoons vegetable oil

1 teaspoon black mustard seeds

1 onion, diced

2 cloves garlic, crushed

1 pound 5 ounces baby leaf spinach

1 tomato, diced

¾ teaspoon salt

¼ teaspoon cayenne pepper

4 eggs

1 teaspoon black peppercorns, coarsely
 crushed

1 tablespoon chopped fresh cilantro

buttered bread or hot naan bread, to serve

This east Indian recipe is traditionally eaten for breakfast, brunch, or lunch with naan bread or "pao", a type of soft bread roll.

Heat the oil in a shallow skillet and fry the mustard seeds until they begin to crackle. Add the onion and garlic and fry until the onion is translucent. Add the spinach, tomato, salt, and cayenne pepper. Cook, covered, over medium heat for 10 minutes, or until the spinach wilts. Stir well and make 4 hollows in the spinach. Break an egg into each hollow. Cover and cook for 10 minutes longer, or until the eggs are set.

Sprinkle with black pepper and fresh cilantro. Lift the eggs and spinach out of the pan, using a flat wooden spoon, and slide onto a plate. Serve with buttered bread or hot naan bread.

TANGY FRUIT SALAD

serves two

1 tablespoon sherry

¼ cup orange juice

1 teaspoon vegetable oil

½ teaspoon cumin seeds

½-inch piece cinnamon stick

4 cloves

4 green cardamom pods

½ pineapple, diced

1 red or green apple, chopped

handful red or green grapes, halved and
   seeded

1 tangerine or orange, segmented

1 green chili, seeded and chopped
   (optional)

pinch of ground nutmeg

This is a good snack if you are bored of eating just plain fruit, and is a good example of how I like to add spice to just about everything! Surprisingly, a seeded green chili mixed in with the fruit gives this salad a pleasant "kick."

Mix the sherry and orange juice together in a large bowl.

Heat the oil in a small skillet and then add the cumin seeds. When they begin to crackle, add the cinnamon stick, cloves, and cardamom pods. Turn off the heat and add this mixture to the sherry and orange juice. Toss in the fruit and the chilli, if using, and sprinkle with nutmeg.

Dinner with the family at the end of the day is a key time for all of us to catch up on everyone's news. Although I am a busy working wife and mother, I strongly believe in the importance of cooking and eating a proper meal with my family. Many people still believe Indian food is time-consuming to prepare as well as being high in fat, but this chapter is full of everyday dishes that are not only quick to prepare, but also provide a balanced diet. Choose from simple fish curries and meat dishes to crunchy vegetables and fresh salads.

everyday family meals

FLAKY FLAT BREAD
WITH A SPICED EGG COATING

serves four

1½ cups all-purpose flour

1½ cups wholewheat flour

1 teaspoon ajowan or cumin seeds

1 tablespoon vegetable oil

⅔ cup warm water

4 eggs, beaten

1 onion, finely chopped

1 tomato, finely chopped

1–2 green chilies, finely chopped

1 tablespoon chopped fresh cilantro

¾ teaspoon salt

3 tablespoons melted butter

lime pickle or tomato catsup, to serve

This is commonly eaten by Indians for breakfast. Indian breads are made fresh every day and we were privileged as children to have a cook who spoiled us and served us the bread as it came hot off the griddle.

Combine the flours in a large bowl. Add the ajowan or cumin seeds. Rub the oil into the flour, then gradually add the water to make a pliable dough. Cover the bowl and let the dough rest for 20 minutes.

In a separate bowl, combine the eggs, onion, tomato, chilies, fresh cilantro, and salt; set aside.

Using your hands, shape the rested dough into 8 balls of equal size. Roll out each ball on a floured board into a flat circle 5 inches in diameter.

Place each paratha on a heated medium-hot griddle or in a large skillet and dry fry for 1–2 minutes on one side, spooning a little melted butter over at the edge. Turn over and cook for 1 minute on the other side, again spooning over a little melted butter at the edges. Flip over once again and spoon 2 tablespoons of the egg mixture on top, followed by ¹/₂ teaspoon of melted butter around the edge. Cook for 1 minute, then flip over and again spoon 2 tablespoons of the egg mixture on top, followed by more melted butter around the edge. Cook until the egg is lightly set.

Serve the parathas hot with lime pickle or tomato catsup.

Tip Shape the dough into 12 rather than 8 balls, if you require smaller parathas. These traditional Indian rolling pins are longer and thinner than Western ones, however, a conventional rolling pin works just as well.

MUSTARD **FISH CURRY**

serves four

5-ounce monkfish steaks

4 tablespoons Dijon mustard

3 tablespoons shredded coconut

2 cloves garlic, crushed

1 tablespoon poppy seeds

1 onion, chopped

1 tablespoon vegetable oil

1 teaspoon black mustard seeds

7 tablespoons canned coconut milk

1 tablespoon ground coriander

2 teaspoons ginger pulp

½ teaspoon salt

½ teaspoon sugar

2 tomatoes, diced

coarsely crushed black mustard seeds
   and watercress leaves, to garnish

This curry, known in India as reshmi rai maach, is absolutely heavenly served with steamed basmati rice and poppadums. The mustard seeds and watercress give it a lovely hot, peppery flavor.

Rub the monkfish steaks all over with the Dijon mustard.

   Place the shredded coconut, garlic, poppy seeds, and onion in a food processor or blender and work until smooth, adding a little water, if necessary, to ease the blending.

   Heat the oil in a pan. Add the mustard seeds and stir until they "pop" then add the blended mixture and fry gently for 2–3 minutes. Add the coconut milk, ground coriander, ginger, salt, and sugar and cook for 10 minutes longer. Add the fish to the pan and cook for 5–8 minutes. Stir in the tomatoes and turn off the heat.

   Sprinkle with coarsely crushed mustard seeds and watercress and serve hot.

AMRITSAR FISH CURRY

serves four

FOR THE BATTER

1 cup chickpea flour (besan)

1 teaspoon garlic pulp

1 teaspoon ground cumin

¼ teaspoon ground black pepper

½ teaspoon ground turmeric

½ teaspoon chili powder

5–7 tablespoons water

FOR THE SAUCE

2 tablespoons vegetable oil

3 black peppercorns

½ teaspoon cumin seeds

2 bay leaves

1 onion, chopped

1 teaspoon garlic pulp

1 teaspoon ground turmeric

1 teaspoon cayenne pepper

1 teaspoon garam masala

3 teaspoons ground coriander

7 ounces tomatoes, chopped

2 green chilies, slit

1 tablespoon tamarind pulp

½ teaspoon sugar

salt

1 tablespoon chopped fresh cilantro

vegetable oil, for deep-frying

11 ounces cod or haddock, cut into
   1½-inch cubes

Amritsar is a north Indian city in Punjab where fish is very seldom eaten—this recipe is a rare exception.

Mix together all the ingredients for the batter until you have a thick batter; set aside.

To make the sauce, heat the oil in a pan and add the black peppercorns, cumin seeds, and bay leaves. When they begin to crackle, add the chopped onions and fry for 5–10 minutes.

Add the garlic pulp, ground turmeric, cayenne pepper, garam masala, and ground coriander and fry for 1 minute. Add the chopped tomatoes and green chilies and continue to cook for 5–10 minutes. Add the tamarind pulp and cook for 5 minutes longer. Lastly, add salt to taste, the sugar, and half the fresh cilantro.

Heat the oil for deep-frying in a large heavy-bottomed pan to 350°F.

Dip each cube of fish into the prepared thick batter, coating it evenly, then drop into the hot oil and deep-fry for about 5 minutes until golden brown.

Arrange the pieces of deep-fried battered fish on a serving dish and pour the sauce over the top. Serve hot, garnished with the remaining fresh cilantro.

FISH IN A TANGY MINTY SAUCE

4 large cod steaks, about 1½ pounds
  total weight

½ teaspoon garam masala

1 teaspoon salt

1¼ pounds chopped fresh cilantro

8–10 small radishes

2 large cloves garlic

2 green chilies, seeded

1 tomato, chopped

12–14 mint leaves

½ teaspoon ginger pulp

1 tablespoon lemon juice

½ teaspoon sugar

1 tablespoon vegetable oil

This is an exceptional dish which is suitable not only as a quick tasty meal on a weekday, but also for entertaining. If you are serving this for a dinner party, you can make the paste for the sauce in advance.

Smear the cod steaks with a mixture of garam masala, salt, and fresh cilantro. Set aside for 12–15 minutes.

Put the remaining ingredients, except the oil, in a food processor or blender and blend to form a smooth paste.

Heat the oil in a deep skillet. Cook the fish on each side for 3–4 minutes, then pour the pureed sauce mixture over the top. Cover and cook for 10 minutes over medium heat. Serve while still hot.

CRISPY COCONUT SHRIMP
WITH TANGY MANGO SAUCE

serves four

2 tablespoons cornstarch

¾ teaspoon salt

½ teaspoon ground black pepper

1 pound 11 ounces raw jumbo shrimp
  (thawed weight if frozen) shelled and
  deveined

2 egg whites, lightly beaten

1 cup shredded coconut

vegetable oil, for deep-frying

FOR THE MANGO SAUCE

1 ripe mango, peeled and chopped

3 tablespoons mayonnaise

3 tablespoons sweet mango chutney

Opposite: **Fish in a tangy minty sauce**

I am always tempted to make this recipe whenever I see jumbo shrimp at my local fishmonger's. It is great as a first course and absolutely delicious as a snack.

Season the cornstarch with the salt and pepper. Dust or toss the shelled shrimp in the cornstarch, then dip each shrimp in the egg white and roll in the shredded coconut.

Heat the oil for deep-frying in a large heavy-bottomed pan to 350°F. While the oil is heating, combine the ingredients for the mango sauce in a blender and work to a puree; place in a serving dish.

When the oil is hot, deep-fry a few shrimp at a time for 2–3 minutes until golden or light brown. Keep warm while you cook the remaining shrimp. Serve hot with the mango sauce.

DRY **SPICED** CHICKEN

serves four

2 tablespoons vegetable oil

1 teaspoon cumin seeds

½ teaspoon fennel seeds

1 bay leaf

2 medium onions, sliced

3 teaspoons ground coriander

1 teaspoon cayenne pepper

1 teaspoon garam masala

1 teaspoon ground turmeric

12 ounces boneless chicken, cut into
   1½-inch pieces

2 green chilies, slit

½ teaspoon black peppercorns, crushed

salt

1 tablespoon chopped fresh cilantro,
   to garnish

This is a great dish for picnics because there is not any sauce so there will be no spillages. It has become a family favorite.

Heat the oil in a pan and add the cumin seeds, fennel seeds, and bay leaf. When they begin to crackle, add the sliced onions and fry for 10–15 minutes over low heat.

Add the ground coriander, cayenne, garam masala, and ground turmeric. Sprinkle with a little water and continue to fry over low heat.

Add the diced chicken and green chilies and fry, stirring continuously. Sprinkle with more water if required. Reduce the heat and cook, covered, for 10–15 minutes.

Add the crushed black peppercorns and salt to taste. Remove the lid and reduce any excess moisture by increasing the heat, stirring all the time. Serve garnished with fresh cilantro.

CHICKEN WITH **PEANUTS**

serves four

½ teaspoon whole fenugreek seeds

2 tablespoons vegetable or sunflower oil

2 pounds chicken thighs or drumsticks, skinned

1 large onion, chopped

1 tablespoon sesame seeds

1 teaspoon freshly cracked black pepper

1 teaspoon ginger pulp

2 large tomatoes, chopped

1 tablespoon ground coriander

½ tablespoon ground cumin

¾ teaspoon ground turmeric

¾ teaspoon cayenne pepper or paprika

7 ounces unsalted peanuts, shelled and skinned

1 teaspoon salt

½ teaspoon sugar

2 tablespoons chopped scallions, to garnish (optional)

Although the Indian state of Gujarat is primarily vegetarian and has a large non-meat-eating community, there still remain some Muslims who eat meat in certain parts of this state. Peanuts, or groundnuts, grow plentifully and are eaten in a variety of dishes. Peanut oil was traditionally used in this recipe, but I use vegetable or sunflower oil instead.

Soak the fenugreek seeds in warm water for 15 minutes.

Heat the oil in a pan, then sear the chicken until brown all over; remove the chicken and drain on paper towels.

In the same oil, fry the onion and cook until translucent. Add the sesame seeds and cook until brown. Add the cracked black pepper, ginger, tomatoes, ground coriander, ground cumin, ground turmeric, cayenne, and peanuts.

Return the chicken to the pan. Cover and cook for 20 minutes; you might need to add a little water if the chicken begins to stick to the pan.

Stir in the salt, sugar, and soaked fenugreek seeds. Serve garnished with chopped scallions, if liked.

SPICED MEAT WITH **SPINACH**

serves four

1 teaspoon vegetable oil

2–4 bay leaves

2–3 black cardamom pods, slightly opened

1 onion, sliced

1 pound ground lamb or beef

½ teaspoon ground turmeric

1 teaspoon ground coriander

1 teaspoon ginger pulp

1 tomato, chopped

1 teaspoon mint sauce, or 4–5 mint leaves

½ teaspoon ground cardamom

1 teaspoon garam masala

1 teaspoon salt

½ teaspoon sugar

10 ounces baby leaf spinach

sliced fried onions, to garnish

Traditionally made with ground lamb or mutton, ground beef is now often substituted in this dish. It is commonly eaten throughout northern India. Serve the dish hot with pilau rice or naan bread.

Heat the oil in a pan. Add the bay leaves and black cardamom pods. After 2–3 seconds, add the sliced onion and cook until translucent. Add the ground meat, reduce the heat, and cook for 10 minutes, stirring to brown the meat evenly. Stir in the ground turmeric, ground coriander, ginger, and tomato.

Continue cooking, covered, for 10 minutes longer. Add the mint sauce or mint leaves, ground cardamom, garam masala, salt, and sugar. Stir well, then fold the whole baby spinach leaves into the meat; cover and cook for 3–4 minutes longer before serving, garnished with sliced fried onions.

GINGERED POTATOES
AND ONIONS

serves four

1 tablespoon vegetable oil

1 teaspoon black mustard seeds

1 teaspoon cumin seeds

1 pound potatoes, peeled and diced

1 onion, cut into large dice

½ teaspoon ground turmeric

1 tablespoon ground coriander

1 teaspoon ground cumin

½ teaspoon cayenne pepper

1-inch piece fresh ginger root,
   peeled and cut into juliennes

1½ teaspoons salt

1 teaspoon sugar

1 tablespoon lemon juice

1 tomato, chopped, to garnish

chopped fresh cilantro, to garnish

This dish is a favorite throughout India, known as garam pyaz aloo. It is served with hot naan bread or chapattis. The heat levels can be reduced by using less cayenne and mustard seeds. Use any leftovers as a sandwich filling the next day—it is wonderful in toasted sandwiches.

Heat the oil in a wok or deep skillet. Add the mustard seeds and stir until they "pop," then add the cumin seeds. When they begin to crackle, add the diced potatoes, onion, and all the ground spices. Cover, reduce the heat, and leave to cook for 12–15 minutes; add a little water if the vegetables start sticking to the pan.

Add the ginger, salt, and sugar to the pan. Stir and cook for 3–4 minutes longer. Turn off the heat—the potatoes should be cooked by now. Stir in the lemon juice.

Garnish the dish with chopped tomato and cilantro leaves and serve.

DEEP-FRIED SPICED
BABY POTATOES

14 ounces new potatoes

vegetable oil, for deep-frying

¼ teaspoon cayenne pepper

1 teaspoon ground roasted cumin seeds
   (see page 22)

juice of ½ lemon

1 tablespoon chopped fresh cilantro

½ teaspoon paprika

½ teaspoon sugar

salt and pepper, to taste (optional)

TO SERVE (OPTIONAL)

natural yogurt

Cilantro and Mint Raita (see page 13)

I make this when I have leftover cooked new potatoes—it makes a very good first course or accompaniment.

If you are using uncooked potatoes, boil them in their skins until they are tender; drain and leave to cool. When cool, hold each potato in your hands and press to flatten slightly.

Heat the oil for deep-frying in a large heavy-bottomed pan to 350°F. Add the potatoes to the hot oil and deep-fry for 10–15 minutes until golden brown and crisp.

Remove from the oil and drain on paper towels. Place in a bowl, add the remaining ingredients to the potatoes, and mix well. Serve hot, drizzled with a little natural yogurt, if liked, and accompanied by Cilantro and Mint Raita.

SPICY SCRAMBLED EGGS

serves four

6 extra-large eggs

¼ cup milk

¼ teaspoon salt

1 tablespoon melted butter

1 tablespoon vegetable oil

1 teaspoon cumin seeds

1 green chili, diced

1 onion, finely diced

½ teaspoon ginger pulp

¼ teaspoon ground turmeric

1 tomato, diced

2 tablespoons chopped fresh cilantro

1 tablespoon grated cheese

This is traditionally eaten for brunch. Originally a Persian dish, it is now served with an Indian "twist". The eggs can be served on top of toast or rolled into warm ready-to-eat chapattis, available from some supermarkets and Asian grocery stores.

Beat the eggs lightly in a bowl with the milk, salt, and melted butter; set aside.

Heat the oil in a wok or deep skillet. Sizzle the cumin seeds in the oil briefly, then add the green chili, onion, ginger, and ground turmeric and fry lightly. Add the tomato and cook for 1–2 minutes longer. Add the egg mixture and cilantro and stir constantly for a few minutes until the eggs are cooked.

Serve the scrambled eggs hot, sprinkled with the grated cheese, on toast or in chapattis.

WHOLE OKRA
STUFFED WITH SPICES

serves four

10 ounces okra

1 teaspoon lemon juice

2 tablespoons vegetable oil

1 tablespoon chopped fresh cilantro, to
   garnish

FOR THE SPICE FILLING

2 tablespoons chickpea flour (besan)

1 teaspoon cayenne pepper

1½ teaspoons salt

1 teaspoon sugar

1 teaspoon ground turmeric

3 teaspoons ground coriander

2 teaspoons ground cumin

⅓ cup crushed peanuts

½ teaspoon asafoetida

This dish is a specialty from the state of Gujarat on the western coast of India. Stuffing okra sounds fussy, but it is really a very simple recipe—the okra are baked in the oven leaving you time to prepare the rest of your meal.

Heat the oven to 350°F.

Clean the okra and make a slit along the length of each.

Mix together all the ingredients for the spice filling in a bowl.

Stuff the slits in the okra with the spice filling, then arrange the stuffed okra on a greased cookie sheet. Sprinkle the okra with the leftover spices, the lemon juice, and the oil and cook in the heated oven for 20–25 minutes until the okra is tender.

Serve hot, sprinkled with chopped fresh cilantro.

GARLIC-FLAVORED LENTILS

serves four

1 cup yellow lentils

½ teaspoon ground turmeric

salt

juice of ½ lemon

1 tablespoon pure ghee

½ teaspoon cumin seeds

3 cloves garlic, chopped

½ teaspoon crushed black peppercorns

2 tablespoons chopped fresh cilantro,
   to garnish

This dal comes from the Parsi community, based around Mumbai and Gujarat. I often eat it with biryani or on its own as a soup.

Wash the lentils in several changes of water. Boil in enough water to cover with the ground turmeric for 20–25 minutes until the lentils are soft; drain and leave to cool.

Place the cooked lentils in a food processor or blender and work to a fine puree: make sure the lentils are of pouring consistency, adding a little more water if required. Reheat the lentil puree and add salt to taste and the lemon juice.

In another small pan, heat the ghee and add the cumin seeds, garlic, and crushed black peppercorns. When they begin to crackle, tip the spices over the lentils and mix well.

Serve the lentils garnished with chopped fresh cilantro.

BABY CORN COBS AND
CRUNCHY GREEN BEANS

serves four

8 ounces green beans

1 teaspoon vegetable oil

1 teaspoon cumin seeds

1 green chili, seeded and chopped

7 ounces baby corn cobs

½ teaspoon ginger pulp

½ teaspoon salt

2 tablespoons water

2 tablespoons shredded coconut

½ teaspoon garam masala

1 tablespoon chopped fresh cilantro

lemon juice, to serve (optional)

Many people think Indian vegetable dishes do not have any texture because of the way vegetables are cooked in many Indian restaurants outside of India. This dish undoes all those preconceptions!

Blanch the beans in a saucepan of boiling water for 2 minutes then drain; slit lengthwise. Top and tail the beans and cut each bean in half.

Heat the oil in a pan, then add the cumin seeds. When they start to crackle, add the green chili. After 30 seconds add the green beans, corn, ginger, and salt; sprinkle with water. Reduce the heat, cover, and cook for 3–4 minutes.

Uncover and sprinkle with the coconut, garam masala, and fresh cilantro. Serve hot while the beans are still "crunchy," sprinkling a little lemon juice on top if liked.

SPINACH WITH CARAMELIZED ONIONS AND GOLDEN RAISINS

serves four

1 tablespoon vegetable oil

4 cloves

1 teaspoon cumin seeds

¼ teaspoon fenugreek seeds

1 red onion, sliced

¾ teaspoon brown sugar

1 tablespoon golden raisins

8 ounces baby spinach

½ teaspoon garam masala

salt

The first time I had this dish was in Agra, home of the Taj Mahal. Both the recipe and one of the most famous wonders of architecture left a lasting memory. If you wish, you can add a dash of cream before sprinkling with garam masala.

Heat the oil in a pan. Add the cloves and when they begin to swell, add the cumin seeds and fenugreek seeds. When they begin to crackle, add the sliced onion and brown sugar. Reduce the heat and cook the onion until brown.

Meanwhile, soak the golden raisins in hot water for 2 minutes; drain and add to the caramelized onions. Fold in the baby spinach, sprinkle with garam masala, and season to taste.

STEAMED FENNEL AND GREEN BEAN VERMICELLI

serves four

8 ounces dried vermicelli, broken into
   2-inch pieces

1 cup sliced thawed frozen green beans

¾ teaspoon garlic pulp

½ teaspoon ginger pulp

½ teaspoon ground turmeric

3 green cardamom pods, cracked open,
   outer pods retained

2 teaspoons fennel seeds

1 onion, sliced

1 green chili, chopped

½ teaspoon vegetable oil

¾ teaspoon sugar

1 teaspoon salt

3–4 cloves

1-inch piece cinnamon stick

2 bay leaves

1 cup water

1 tablespoon chopped fresh cilantro

This accompaniment, known as saunf aur sem ki seviyan, is quite an unusual dish, and one not normally seen in Indian restaurants outside of India. I first tasted it in Baroda, a city in the state of Gujarat. It is a healthy option for those who are watching their weight.

Combine all the ingredients together in a large bowl and then place in a steaming basket or colander, large enough to fit inside a pressure cooker; steam for 20–25 minutes. The vermicelli should absorb all the water.

   Alternatively, put all the ingredients in a large glass bowl, cover, and cook in the microwave on High for 15 minutes, or until all the water is absorbed and the vermicelli is tender.

   Serve while still hot.

SPICY COUSCOUS SALAD

serves four

1 cup couscous

10–12 cherry tomatoes, halved

3-inch piece cucumber, sliced

1 red onion, sliced

1 green chili, seeded

¾ teaspoon toasted cumin seeds

1 tablespoon chopped fresh cilantro

2 tablespoons lemon juice

½ teaspoon sugar

1 teaspoon salt

½ teaspoon ground black pepper

1 teaspoon olive, vegetable or sesame oil

Couscous has been eaten for several years in India, but never in a salad. I experimented with leftover couscous to make this salad and was delighted with the result.

For an alternative version to the one below, drizzle the whole cherry tomatoes and the red onion with the oil and a little salt and roast in a preheated oven, 450°F, for 8–10 minutes. Add to the couscous along with the juices from the roasting pan and the remaining ingredients.

Cook the couscous according to the package directions. Transfer to a large bowl and add all the remaining ingredients. Stir well to combine and serve at room temperature.

SPICED RICE

serves four

1¼ cups basmati rice

3 tablespoons oil

¼ teaspoon cumin seeds

3 cloves

2 bay leaves

3 green cardamom pods

2 onions, sliced

1 tablespoon garlic pulp

½ teaspoon ground turmeric

½ teaspoon cayenne pepper

3 teaspoons ground coriander

1½ cups chopped tomatoes

1½ teaspoons garam masala

2 tablespoons chopped fresh cilantro

salt

This spiced fragrant rice is a lunchtime dish, but it can also be eaten as an accompaniment. Serve with natural yogurt.

Wash the rice in several changes of water, then leave to soak for 10 minutes before draining well.

Heat the oil in a pan and add the cumin seeds, cloves, bay leaves, and cardamom pods. When they begin to crackle, add the sliced onions and fry over medium heat for 5 minutes.

Add the garlic pulp and the ground turmeric, cayenne, and ground coriander. Sprinkle with a little water and continue to cook over low heat, stirring frequently. Add the tomatoes and continue to cook for 4–5 minutes. When the oil separates from the other ingredients, add the drained soaked rice. Add the garam masala and fresh cilantro and pour enough hot water into the pan to a level $1/2$ inch above the layer of rice. Add salt to taste and leave to cook over medium heat.

When the water begins to boil, cover the pan. Reduce the heat and simmer for 10–12 minutes until the rice is cooked.

Opposite: **Spicy couscous salad**

TANGY CIRCLES OF **EGGPLANT**

serves four

2 large purple eggplants, sliced into ½ inch
  thick rounds

1 teaspoon salt

1 tablespoon ground coriander

1 tablespoon ground cumin

¼ teaspoon ground turmeric

1 teaspoon garlic pulp

2 tablespoons vegetable oil

1 teaspoon black mustard seeds

TO GARNISH

1 teaspoon roasted coriander seeds,
  ground

2 teaspoons chopped fresh cilantro

1 teaspoon lemon juice

As a child khat mith baingan pati was one of my favorite dishes—we used to beg to have this throughout November and December as this was the only time of year that eggplants were available. Now I can cook it any time—I like to serve it with parathas (see page 12) or natural yogurt.

Sprinkle the eggplant slices with the salt and set aside for 10–15 minutes. Gently squeeze each eggplant slice between the palms of your hands to remove all remaining moisture.

Mix together the ground coriander, cumin, ground turmeric, and garlic pulp, then sprinkle on both sides of the eggplant.

Heat the oil in a wok. Add the mustard seeds and stir until they "pop" then layer the eggplant in the pan, making sure each slice is slightly covered with the mustard oil.

Cook for 3–4 minutes on one side, then gently turn over with a spatula to cook the other side: do not cover the pan. Reduce the heat and cook for 5 minutes: turn off the heat.

Serve, sprinkled with ground roasted coriander, fresh cilantro, and lemon juice.

BEAN SPROUT AND PEANUT SALAD

serves four

1 teaspoon salt

1 pound 12 ounces bean sprouts

⅔ cup shelled peanuts, or 7 ounces
   snow peas or green beans

1 teaspoon tamarind pulp

2 tablespoons hot water

1 teaspoon vegetable oil

2 tablespoons sesame seeds

1 green chili, seeded and chopped

1 tablespoon coarsely ground pepper

1 teaspoon ginger pulp

2 tablespoons chopped fresh cilantro

salt and pepper, to taste

½ red onion, finely sliced, to garnish

This healthy salad is delicious eaten hot or cold. If you are allergic to nuts or on a diet, you can replace the peanuts with snow peas or whole green beans. Although bean sprouts are most often used in Chinese cooking, they are also used in northern parts of India.

Bring a large saucepan of salted water to a boil. Add the bean sprouts and blanch for 2–3 minutes. Remove from the water using a slotted spoon and place in a large bowl.

Blanch the peanuts or green vegetables in the same water for 5 minutes; drain, then add to the bowl of bean sprouts.

Stir the tamarind pulp and 2 tablespoons of hot water together to form a smooth paste; set aside for 2–3 minutes.

Meanwhile, heat the oil in a pan, then add the sesame seeds. When they start to crackle, add the green chili and stir briefly. Add these spices to the bean sprouts, then stir in the pepper, ginger, tamarind, and fresh cilantro. Toss the salad and season to taste. Eat hot or cold, garnished with slices of red onion.

INDIAN **CARROT** PUDDING

serves four

2 tablespoons ghee

6–8 broken unsalted cashew nuts

10–12 raisins

2¼ pounds carrots, peeled and grated

1 quart milk

⅓ cup sugar

few drops of vanilla extract

pistachio slivers, to decorate

Known as gajjar halwa, this is India's favorite halwa (pudding). It can also be made with doodhi, a large Indian zucchini.

Heat the ghee in a pan and fry the cashew nuts and raisins over low-to-medium heat. When they begin to color add the grated carrots and fry for about 5 minutes until the carrots are soft. Add the milk and bring to a boil, stirring well.

When the milk begins to boil, add the sugar. Reduce the heat to a simmer for 15–20 minutes, by which time the milk will reduce and the carrots become mushy. Add the vanilla extract, turn off the heat, and stir well. Serve either hot or cold, decorated with pistachio slivers.

easy
entertaining

For me sitting down to enjoy some good food in the company

of friends is one of life's greatest pleasures. This chapter is about

simple entertaining, and includes some of my favorite recipes.

Some of the ingredients are a little more special, while others,

such as the spiced puffed bread, look fantastically impressive

but are delicious recipes that can be prepared with the

minimum of fuss.

MONKFISH WITH MUSHROOMS

serves four (as an appetizer)

1 tablespoon butter

4 cloves garlic, sliced

1 teaspoon ginger pulp

8–10 scallions, chopped

1 green bell pepper, seeded and sliced

1 teaspoon cayenne pepper

1 teaspoon salt

11 ounces monkfish, cut into 1½-inch
  cubes

12 raw jumbo shrimp, thawed if frozen,
  shelled and deveined

⅔ cup thickly sliced mushrooms

2 tablespoons light cream

pinch of sugar

crushed black peppercorns, to garnish

I absolutely adore this appetizer. Monkfish and mushrooms both have a "meaty" texture and they complement each other well. Serve with a salad and some warm bread.

Melt the butter in a skillet. Add the garlic, ginger, scallions, green pepper, cayenne, and salt. Stir-fry for 3–4 minutes, then add the monkfish and shrimp. Reduce the heat and continue frying for 5–7 minutes.

Add the mushrooms, cream, and sugar. Cover the pan and simmer for 3–4 minutes. Sprinkle with crushed black pepper and serve hot.

FISH IN FENNEL AND CREAM

serves four

1½ tablespoons vegetable oil

6 tablespoons heavy cream

¾ teaspoon salt

4 cloves garlic, finely crushed

1 tablespoon finely chopped fresh
  cilantro

pinch of ground nutmeg

¼ teaspoon ground turmeric

4 x 5–6 ounce cod steaks

FOR THE PANCH POORAN SPICES

5 dried red chilies

1 teaspoon black mustard seeds

½ teaspoon fenugreek seeds

1½ tablespoons fennel seeds

1½ teaspoons cumin seeds

Panch pooran is a spice blend from Bengal with a powerful aroma. This east Indian delicacy will leave your taste buds tingling. The leftover panch pooran spices can be stored in an airtight container for up to six months. Serve the fish with rice and Mixed Vegetable Raita (see page 14).

Begin by mixing together all the panch pooran spices.

Place 1¹/₂ tablespoons of the prepared panch pooran spices in a bowl. Add the vegetable oil, heavy cream, salt, garlic, fresh cilantro, nutmeg, and ground turmeric and mix well to form a paste. Rub this paste on both sides of the fish steaks and arrange the fish on a greased cookie sheet.

Place the fish under a heated broiler and broil on one side for 5 minutes. Turn the fish over using a spatula and broil the other side for 3–4 minutes. Serve at once.

SHRIMP WITH SPINACH

2 tablespoons vegetable oil

½ teaspoon cumin seeds

2 bay leaves

1 large onion, chopped

1½ teaspoons ginger pulp

4 cloves garlic, chopped

1 teaspoon ground turmeric

2 green chilies, chopped

½ teaspoon cayenne pepper

2 tomatoes, diced

12 ounces raw jumbo shrimp, shelled and
   deveined

2¾ cups shredded spinach

1½ teaspoons garam masala

2 tablespoons light cream

salt

2 tablespoons chopped fresh cilantro

Leafy vegetables, like the spinach in this recipe, are often combined with fish and meat in both the north and south of India. This is a great dish for entertaining—especially if you have guests who don't eat meat.

Heat the oil in a pan and add the cumin seeds and bay leaves. When they begin to crackle, add the chopped onion and fry for 5–8 minutes.

Add the ginger pulp, garlic, ground turmeric, and green chilies and continue to fry. Add the cayenne and diced tomatoes. After 2 minutes add the shelled shrimp and cook for 5 minutes.

Add the shredded spinach, cover, and leave to steam for 5 minutes to soften the spinach; stir well. Add the garam masala and light cream and season to taste.

Stir in the chopped fresh cilantro and serve.

SHRIMP IN SWEET LIME CURRY WITH MANDARIN ORANGES

serves four

2 tablespoons butter

3 tablespoons vegetable oil

1 onion, very finely chopped

3 cloves garlic, chopped

1 teaspoon ginger pulp

1 tablespoon ground coriander

1 teaspoon garam masala

6–8 curry leaves (optional)

2 chilies, finely chopped

2¼ pounds large raw jumbo shrimp with
   tails on, shelled and deveined

2 tablespoons sweet lime pickle

7 tablespoons dry white wine

1 can (11-oz.) mandarin orange
   segments in juice, drained

salt

roughly chopped dill, to garnish

This is another great dish for a dinner party as the sauce can be made a day ahead. Simply add cooked shrimp and heat through.

Melt the butter with the oil in a pan and fry the onion, garlic, and ginger for 8–10 minutes until the onion is translucent.

Add the ground coriander, garam masala, curry leaves, and green chilies and continue cooking for 3–5 minutes. Add the shrimp and cook, stirring gently, for 5 minutes. Stir in the lime pickle, dry white wine, and drained mandarins. Adjust the seasoning to taste and cook for 3–5 minutes longer, or until the sauce begins to thicken.

Serve the curry hot on a bed of plain steamed or boiled rice, garnished with dill.

Tip I find that a pinch of salt and sugar highlight the flavor.

BAKED GARLIC AND CHILI CHEESE OYSTERS

serves four (as a starter)

16 oysters, opened in their half shells

2 tablespoons butter

2 scallions (including green shoots),
   chopped

1 clove garlic, crushed

1 teaspoon very finely chopped fresh
   cilantro

2 teaspoons grated mild cheddar or any
   blue-veined cheese, if preferred

1½ teaspoon cayenne pepper

The Indian name for this dish, samundar ka kamaal, always brings a smile to my face. Samundar means "sea" and kamaal means "fascination" or "wonder."

Heat the oven to 300°F.

Rinse the oysters in cold water and place in a baking dish.

Melt the butter in a pan and add the scallions, garlic, and cilantro. Mix well.

Spoon the scallion mixture over the oysters. Sprinkle with the cheese and cayenne, then bake for 5–8 minutes, or until the cheese starts to melt. Serve hot.

CHICKEN IN A STRONG **GARLIC SAUCE**

3 tablespoons vegetable oil

2 cloves

2 green cardamom pods

1-inch piece cinnamon stick

½ teaspoon cumin seeds

1 large onion, sliced

2 teaspoons ginger pulp

3 teaspoons garlic pulp

½ teaspoon ground turmeric

½ teaspoon cayenne pepper

1½ teaspoons ground coriander

1½ cups chopped tomatoes

14 ounces boneless chicken, cut into
   1–1½-inch cubes

2 tablespoons light cream

1 teaspoon garam masala

salt

5 cloves garlic, sliced

2 tablespoons chopped fresh cilantro, to
   garnish

This chicken dish is a real must for garlic lovers! Garlic is believed to have great curative powers, from aiding digestion to guarding against infectious diseases.

Heat 2 tablespoons oil in a pan and add the cloves, cardamom pods, cinnamon, and cumin seeds. When they begin to crackle, add the sliced onions and fry for 5–10 minutes. Add the ginger, garlic, ground turmeric, cayenne, and ground coriander, reduce the heat, and fry for 8–10 minutes.

Add the chopped tomatoes and continue to cook over low to medium heat for 10–15 minutes.

Add the diced chicken and continue to cook for 10 minutes: sprinkle with a little water if the chicken is sticking to the pan. Add the light cream and simmer for 5 minutes. Add salt to taste and sprinkle with garam masala.

In another pan, heat the remaining 1 tablespoon oil and fry the sliced garlic over medium heat for 2–3 minutes until it turns golden brown. Add to the chicken and serve the dish garnished with fresh cilantro.

CHICKEN STUFFED WITH CASHEW NUTS, CHEESE, AND PEAS

⅔ cup cashew nuts, chopped or
  coarsely ground

7 ounces ricotta cheese

1 teaspoon cumin seeds

1 teaspoon garam masala

1 red onion, finely diced

⅔ cup thawed frozen peas

½ teaspoon cracked black pepper

1 green chili, seeded and finely chopped

½ teaspoon salt

4 skinned boneless chicken breast halves

FOR THE SAUCE

2 tablespoons butter

4 cloves

4 bay leaves

1-inch piece cinnamon stick

1 onion, chopped

1 teaspoon ginger pulp

1 teaspoon finely chopped garlic

11 ounces canned crushed tomatoes

½ teaspoon ground turmeric

¼ teaspoon cayenne pepper (optional)

½ teaspoon salt

1 teaspoon sugar

½ teaspoon garam masala

7 tablespoons light cream

The stuffing for this Indo-Persian dish can be made in advance and stored in the refrigerator until required.

Mix the cashew nuts, ricotta cheese, cumin seeds, garam masala, red onion, peas, black peppercorns, chili, and salt together in a bowl.

Flatten the chicken breasts using a rolling pin or wooden mallet, then spread a quarter of the nut mixture over each. Roll up each breast and secure with a wooden toothpick or with meat string tied around each breast.

To make the sauce, melt the butter in a shallow pan and add the cloves, bay leaves, and cinnamon stick. When the cloves begin to "swell", add the onion, ginger, and garlic and sauté for 5–7 minutes. Add the rolled stuffed chicken breasts to the pan and brown on all sides. Add a little water and cover the pan. Reduce the heat and cook for 15 minutes.

Add the tomatoes, ground turmeric, cayenne, salt, sugar, and garam masala and let the chicken and tomato sauce simmer for 10–12 minutes longer, or until chicken is completely cooked through and the juices run clear.

Gently stir in the cream and serve the chicken hot with warm naan bread.

CHICKEN IN ALMOND SAUCE

serves four

4 ounces slivered almonds, plus extra to
  garnish

2 tablespoons vegetable oil

1 teaspoon cumin seeds

3 cloves

3 green cardamom pods

1 teaspoon garlic pulp

½ teaspoon ground turmeric

2 bay leaves

1 large onion, chopped

12 ounces boneless chicken, cut into
  1–1½-inch cubes

¼ cup light cream

1 teaspoon ground cardamom

1 teaspoon garam masala

1 teaspoon sugar

salt

1 tablespoon chopped fresh cilantro, to
  garnish

This is a great favorite with all my dinner guests, who often request this dish when they are invited around—the fragrant creamy sauce is delicious. Serve with Spiced Kidney Beans with Ginger and Yogurt (see page 66).

Soak the slivered almonds in warm water for a couple of hours. Drain and then process in a food processor or blender to a fine puree; set aside.

Heat the oil in a pan and add the cumin seeds, cloves, cardamom pods, garlic pulp, ground turmeric, and bay leaves. When the spices begin to crackle, add the chopped onions and fry for 5–10 minutes.

Add the diced chicken and continue to fry, stirring continuously. Stir in the prepared almond puree and cook over a low to medium heat for 15–20 minutes.

Stir in the light cream, ground cardamom, and garam masala. Add the sugar and salt to taste. Cook for 3–5 minutes longer. Serve at once, garnished with a few almond slivers and chopped fresh cilantro.

Tip Why not try this recipe using other nuts? Pistachios, cashew nuts, pinenuts, and chestnuts all work well and give completely different flavors.

easy entertaining

PORK WITH
PICKLING SPICES

serves four

1 tablespoon vegetable oil

**2-inch piece fresh ginger root, peeled
and finely sliced**

4 cloves garlic, finely chopped

**1 pound pork tenderloin, cut into 1-inch
strips**

2 tablespoons sweet mango chutney

2 tablespoons hot lime pickle

**2 tablespoons diagonally cut green shoots
of scallion**

1 teaspoon chopped fresh cilantro

*This north Indian recipe lends itself to both special occasions
and everyday cooking. It can be made with either pork or lamb.
If using lamb, get the butcher to cut the meat from the leg into
strips for you. Serve the meat with plain boiled basmati rice
and lentils.*

Heat the oil in a wok and slowly fry the ginger and garlic for
1–2 minutes. Add the pork and stir-fry for 8–10 minutes. Add
the mango chutney and hot lime pickle.

Cover the pan, reduce the heat, and cook for 5 minutes; add
a little water if the meat begins to stick. Turn off the heat, stir
in the scallions and chopped fresh cilantro and serve.

LAMB LIVER
BAKED WITH **FENNEL**

serves four

2 tablespoons vegetable oil

1¼ pound lamb liver, cut into strips

2 tablespoons fennel seeds

¾ ounce creamed coconut

¼ cup water

6 cloves garlic

1 small onion, finely chopped

1 teaspoon ginger pulp

¼ teaspoon ground turmeric

¼ teaspoon black mustard seeds,
   coarsely crushed

¼ teaspoon asafoetida (optional)

¾ teaspoon salt

Liver is not commonly eaten in India, but this dish is a delicacy from the 1930s, which I was lucky enough to discover at a friend's house. Serve hot with green beans.

Heat the oven to 350°F.

Heat the oil in a shallow skillet. Sear the liver strips for 5–8 minutes; set aside.

Dry-fry the fennel seeds in a hot skillet for 2 minutes, tossing them continuously. Coarsely crush them with a rolling pin.

Combine the creamed coconut with the water and garlic. Boil in a pan for 5 minutes, then put the mixture in a blender and work to a puree. Put the seared liver, the crushed fennel seeds, the coconut puree, and all the remaining ingredients in a baking dish. Cover with foil and bake in the oven for 25 minutes. Serve while still hot.

SPICED **KIDNEY BEANS**
WITH GINGER AND YOGURT

serves four

1 tablespoon vegetable oil or ghee

1-inch piece cinnamon stick

1 cup natural yogurt

1 teaspoon ginger pulp

8–10 green cardamom pods, crushed

¼ teaspoon ground turmeric

1 pound 5 ounces can kidney beans,
   drained

1½ teaspoons salt

¾ teaspoon cayenne pepper

1 large tomato, chopped

TO GARNISH

1 tablespoon chopped fresh cilantro

1 tablespoon chopped onion

This rustic dish, known as rajma, is popular among all north Indian families, especially the farming community. It is a delicious accompaniment to Chicken in Almond Sauce (see page 62), or serve it simply with plain rice or naan bread and poppadums.

Heat the oil or ghee in a pan. Add the cinnamon stick and stir. After 2–3 seconds, add the natural yogurt, ginger, crushed cardamom pods, and ground turmeric. Cook over medium heat, stirring constantly, for 10 minutes.

Add the remaining ingredients and cook for 15 minutes. Garnish with chopped cilantro and onion and serve.

LAMB AND POTATO CURRY

serves four

- 2 tablespoons vegetable oil
- 2 cloves
- 2 green cardamom pods
- 2 teaspoons ground black pepper
- 2 bay leaves
- 1 teaspoon cumin seeds
- 1 large onion, sliced
- 7 ounces chopped tomatoes
- 1 teaspoon ground turmeric
- 1 teaspoon cayenne pepper
- 1 teaspoon garam masala
- 3 teaspoons ground coriander
- 12 ounces boneless lamb, cut into 1½-inch cubes
- 15 cup potato cut into sticks
- ¼ cup natural yogurt
- salt
- chopped fresh cilantro, to garnish

Gosht aloo (lamb with potato) is an authentic recipe that is commonly eaten by non-vegetarian Indians, however, I have adapted it by adding a little yogurt to tone down the heat.

Heat the oil in a pan and add the cloves, cardamom pods, black pepper, bay leaves, and cumin seeds. When they begin to crackle, add the sliced onions and fry for 10–15 minutes over medium heat until they turn translucent.

Add the chopped tomatoes, ground turmeric, cayenne, garam masala, and ground coriander and continue to fry for 5 minutes longer.

Stir in the diced lamb, potato sticks, and natural yogurt. Add salt to taste and cook, covered, over low heat for 20–25 minutes.

Serve hot, garnished with chopped fresh cilantro.

BABY CORN AND MUSHROOMS IN A SPICY TOMATO AND ONION SAUCE

serves four

2 tablespoons vegetable oil

½ teaspoon cumin seeds

1-inch piece fresh ginger root, chopped

1 green chili, chopped

1 teaspoon ground turmeric

1 large onion, chopped

1 tablespoon garlic pulp

½ teaspoon cayenne pepper

2 teaspoons ground coriander

1½ cups chopped tomatoes

1 teaspoon cumin seeds

1 teaspoon coriander seeds

1 teaspoon fennel seeds

½ teaspoon cracked black pepper

1 dried red chili, chopped

1 teaspoon sugar

salt

5 ounces baby corn cobs, blanched for
    2 minutes in boiling water and then cut
    lengthwise

5 ounces button mushrooms, blanched for
    2 minutes in boiling water and then
    quartered

1 tablespoon light cream

1 tablespoon chopped fresh cilantro

This is known as tawa makai khumbh in India—a tawa is a heavy cast-iron griddle, traditionally used to make Indian breads like chapattis. This recipe has been adapted, however, so that it can be cooked in a wok or pan. This makes a good vegetarian main dish served with rice or bread, but I also like to eat it as an accompaniment to other dishes.

Heat the oil in a pan or wok and add the cumin seeds. When they begin to crackle, add the chopped ginger, green chili, ground turmeric, and onion in sequence and fry over medium heat for 10 minutes.

Add the garlic pulp, cayenne, ground coriander, and chopped tomatoes and continue to cook for 5–10 minutes longer.

Meanwhile, in another pan, dry-fry the cumin seeds, coriander seeds, fennel seeds, black pepper, and chopped red chili over low heat for 5 minutes. Transfer these spices to a mortar and crush to a coarse mix using the pestle. Sprinkle this mixture into the tomato sauce.

Add the sugar to the tomato sauce and salt to taste, then add the baby corn and mushrooms. Pour in the cream and cook for 2–3 minutes longer. Stir in the fresh coriander and serve.

EGGPLANTS AND POTATOES

serves four

2 tablespoons vegetable oil

½ teaspoon cumin seeds

1 teaspoon ginger pulp

1 green chili, chopped

4–5 curry leaves

½ teaspoon ground turmeric

½ teaspoon cayenne pepper

¼ teaspoon asafoetida

2½ cups chopped tomatoes

1 cup diced potatoes

1 cup eggplant, diced

salt

1 teaspoon sugar

1 tablespoon natural yogurt

chopped fresh cilantro, to garnish

I love eggplants and have a whole collection of recipes for this wonderful vegetable.

Heat the oil in a pan and add the cumin seeds. When they begin to crackle, add the ginger pulp, green chili, and curry leaves. After 1 minute add the ground turmeric, cayenne, and asafoetida. Reduce the heat and sprinkle with a little water.

After about 2 minutes add the chopped tomatoes and bring to a boil. Add the potatoes and eggplant and cook, covered, at a simmer for 5–10 minutes: check that the potatoes are tender. Add salt to taste, then stir in the sugar and yogurt.

Serve garnished with chopped fresh cilantro.

TAMARIND RICE

serves four

1¼ cups basmati rice

3 tablespoons vegetable oil

2 tablespoons black mustard seeds

8–10 curry leaves

2 dry whole red chilies

1½ teaspoons asafoetida (optional)

2 tablespoons sesame seeds

1½ teaspoons ginger pulp

½ teaspoon ground turmeric

1 teaspoon salt

3 cups water

2 tablespoons tamarind pulp

1 cup drained canned chickpeas,
   coarsely crushed

The combination of rice and tamarind pulp easily gives away that this is a dish from southern India. It is commonly served with fish dishes.

Wash the rice in several changes of water, then leave to soak for 10 minutes before draining well.

Heat the oil in a large pan and fry the mustard seeds until they begin to crackle. Add the curry leaves, whole red chilies, asafoetida, and sesame seeds. As the sesame seeds begin to brown, add the drained soaked rice, ginger, and ground turmeric. Add the salt and water and bring to a boil.

Stir the tamarind pulp and crushed chickpeas into the rice mixture. Cover the pan and simmer for 15–20 minutes, or until the rice is cooked. Serve at once.

Opposite: **Eggplants and potatoes**

SPICED DEEP-FRIED PURIS

serves four

2¾ cups wholewheat flour

½ teaspoon salt

1 tablespoon vegetable oil

½ teaspoon ground turmeric

1 teaspoon ajowan seeds

½ teaspoon cayenne pepper

⅔ cup warm water

vegetable oil, for deep-frying

mango chutney, to serve

Puris are delicious rounds of dough that puff up when deep-fried. I often eat these as a snack with mango chutney, but I also enjoy serving them to guests as they look very impressive.

Combine the flour and salt in a bowl and mix well. Rub the oil into the flour, then stir in the ground turmeric, ajowan seeds, and cayenne pepper. Slowly add the warm water into the spiced flour until it forms a pliable dough. Cover the bowl and set aside for 15–20 minutes.

Divide the rested dough mixture into 16 balls. Roll out each ball on a lightly floured surface into a 4-inch circle.

Heat the oil for deep-frying in a large, heavy-bottomed pan until it is nearly smoking hot—470°F. Once hot, reduce the heat to medium, about 350°F.

Immerse each puri, one at a time, in the hot oil. Gently push into the oil with a slotted spoon and leave to "puff up," which happens almost immediately. Turn once and cook the other side for 1–2 seconds. Using the slotted spoon, remove the puri from the pan and place on paper towels to drain while you cook the remaining puris.

Eat the puris while still puffed, with sweet mango chutney or any meat or vegetable dish.

SPINACH AND CHICKPEA FLOUR BREAD

serves four

2½ cups chickpea flour (besan)

⅓ cup all-purpose flour

½ cup shredded spinach

½ teaspoon cumin seeds

½-inch piece fresh ginger root,
   chopped

1 green chili, chopped

1 tablespoon chopped fresh cilantro

1 teaspoon ground turmeric

pinch of salt

4 tablespoons vegetable oil

This flat spiced bread with bright speckles of green spinach comes from the central states of India. Some people like to eat roti as soon as they are cooked, but I prefer them at room temperature.

Mix the chickpea flour in a bowl with the all-purpose flour and add all the other ingredients, except the oil. Add enough water to make a thick dough. Use your hands to work the spinach well into the dough.

Divide the dough into 8 and roll out each piece on a floured board into a flat circle 5–6 inches in diameter.

Heat a crepe pan or griddle. Cook the flat breads one at a time for 2–3 minutes on one side then turn over and cook the other side. Drizzle with oil and continue to cook until the breads are well done, turning the bread over frequently during cooking.

BEET PUDDING

1 cup boiled diced beet

1 quart milk

½ cup sugar

1 tablespoon rice flour

2 tablespoons ghee

10–12 raisins

10–15 unsalted cashew nuts, roughly chopped

few drops of rose extract

rose petals, to decorate

You would probably never imagine combining milk with beet, but it makes a vibrant dessert and looks lovely when decorated with rose petals.

Place the boiled beet in a food processor. Add a little water and blend to a fine puree.

Pour the milk into a saucepan and bring to a boil. Reduce the heat and simmer for 15–20 minutes. Add the sugar and stir well to dissolve it.

Mix the rice flour in a cup with a little water to make a paste. Add this paste to the milk, stirring the mixture continuously as it starts to thicken.

In another pan, melt the ghee and add the raisins and cashew nuts. Fry for 1–2 minutes. Add the beet puree and cook for 10–12 minutes over low heat.

Pour the beet mixture into the thickened milk and mix well to obtain an even pink color. Add the rose extract and pour into 4 individual dessert bowls.

Serve chilled, decorated with a few rose petals.

COOL **MANGO** SOUP

makes 1 ¾ quarts

4 large semiripe mangoes

1½ quarts water

8–10 tablespoons brown sugar

1 tablespoon ginger pulp

1 teaspoon ground black pepper

1 teaspoon chat masala (see page 122)

1 teaspoon coarsely crushed roasted
   cumin seeds (see page 22)

1 teaspoon salt, or to taste

Mangoes are Indians' favorite fruit and we try to make as many recipes with them as possible during the mango season, which, in India, runs from March through May. They are grown in abundance in Mumbai, where I grew up.

This recipe is a drink or soup, which is mainly prepared in Gujarat households and sipped throughout the sultry heat of the day to keep cool. Once made, it keeps for up to 4 days in the refrigerator.

Peel the mangoes and cut them into big chunks: do not discard the seeds.

Boil the mango pieces and seeds in the water for 15 minutes, or until the mango turns pulpy; leave to cool.

Discard the mango seeds. Put the mango flesh in a blender and work to a puree. Return to the saucepan and bring back to a boil. Add the remaining ingredients.

The "soup" is best served chilled with ice or at room temperature.

Tip Add a little extra sugar if the raw mangoes are very "tangy."

home
comforts

Some days I just want to curl up on the sofa and indulge in some comfort food. For me, this can be anything from a bowl of spicy pumpkin soup to a delicious, warming dal. In this chapter I have included some of my family's favorite dishes, from the dry spiced cabbage dish my daughter loves to fried sweet potatoes with ice cream. Enjoy.

CHICKPEA FLOUR "CREPES"

serves four

2¼ cups chickpea flour (besan)

pinch of salt

½ teaspoon ground turmeric

¼ teaspoon baking soda

½ teaspoon ground cumin

1 tablespoon natural yogurt

1 onion, finely chopped

1 green chili, finely chopped

2 tomatoes, diced

1 tablespoon chopped fresh cilantro

4–5 tablespoons vegetable oil

Known as cheela, these thick "crepes" are eaten throughout northern and central India, both as a breakfast dish and as a snack with pickles and mango chutney.

Put the flour in a bowl. Add the salt, ground turmeric, baking soda, ground cumin, yogurt, and enough water to make a slightly thick, flowing batter. Stir in the chopped onion, green chili, tomatoes, and cilantro.

Heat a nonstick 5-inch crepe pan. Pour in a little of the batter, spreading it to cover the bottom completely and make a thin crepe. Drizzle 1 teaspoon oil over the top.

Reduce the heat and continue to cook the crepe for 2–3 minutes. Flip the crepe over and cook the other side for 2–3 minutes. Remove from the pan and keep warm while you make another 7 crepes in the same way. Serve hot.

MEENA PATHAK'S
PUMPKIN SOUP

serves four

1 tablespoon butter

4 scallions, finely chopped

**1½ pounds pumpkin, peeled and cut
into ¾-inch cubes**

2 carrots, diced

1 teaspoon salt

¾ teaspoon ground black pepper

¼ teaspoon ground green cardamom

¼ teaspoon ground cinnamon

¼ teaspoon ground cloves

pinch of ground nutmeg

1¼ cups vegetable stock

7 tablespoons milk

¼ cup light cream

**2 tablespoons finely chopped dill leaves,
to garnish**

Often called "MKP's Pumpkin Soup" in my family, this came about when I was trying to use up some leftover vegetables in the refrigerator. It has become the family's favorite soup.

Melt the butter in a large saucepan. Add the scallions and fry for 3–4 minutes.

Add the pumpkin, carrots, salt, all the ground spices, and stock. Bring to a boil. Cook until the carrots and pumpkin are tender—10–15 minutes.

Leave the mixture to cool slightly before putting it in a blender. Give it a couple of bursts of power, but do not puree it completely.

Return the soup to the pan. Add the milk and bring back to a boil. Stir in the cream, adjust the seasoning to taste, and serve hot, garnished with dill leaves.

EASY BROILED CHICKEN BITES

1 tablespoon paprika

2 teaspoons garam masala

1½ teaspoons salt

1 teaspoon sugar

1 tablespoon vegetable oil, plus extra for drizzling

1 tablespoon garlic pulp

1 tablespoon natural yogurt

9 ounces boneless, skinless chicken breast halves, cut into bite-size pieces

TO GARNISH

onion, cut into rings

1 tablespoon chopped fresh cilantro

few sprigs of mint

This is a classic appetizer you would expect to find in a north Indian non-vegetarian household—however I often make these as a snack for my family.

Combine all the ingredients, except the chicken, together in a bowl and stir well. Add the chicken and stir well, making sure the marinade coats all the chicken pieces; set aside to marinate for a few minutes.

Place the chicken pieces in a broiler pan and drizzle with a little oil. Place under a heated medium-hot broiler and broil for 5–8 minutes until golden brown. Turn the pieces over and cook the other side for 5 minutes longer.

When cooked, remove and arrange on a plate. Serve with onion rings, chopped cilantro, and mint sprigs.

DEVILED SHRIMPS

serves four

1 tablespoon vegetable oil

1 onion, finely chopped

2 cloves garlic, finely chopped

¾ teaspoon cayenne pepper

1 teaspoon paprika

¼ teaspoon ground black pepper

¼ teaspoon ground turmeric

½ teaspoon grated fresh ginger root

1 teaspoon salt

1¾ pounds shelled raw shrimp (thawed weight if frozen)

⅔ cup water

1 tablespoon tomato catsup

These delicious spicy shrimp are great for cold wintry nights. Serve the shrimp hot with naan bread or on crackers with Coriander and Mint Raita (see page 13).

Heat the oil in a wok or heavy-bottomed skillet. Add the onion and cook until golden brown. Add the garlic, cayenne, paprika, black pepper, ground turmeric, ginger, and salt and cook, stirring, for 2–3 minutes.

Add the shrimp and cook for 5 minutes, then add the water, cover, and bring to a boil. Stir in the tomato catsup and cook, uncovered, for 2–3 minutes, before serving hot.

TANDOORI
BROILED VEGETABLES

serves four

1 large green bell pepper, seeded and
  sliced

1 large red bell pepper, seeded and sliced

4 large tomatoes, sliced

1 large onion, sliced

2 zucchini, sliced

10–12 mushrooms

1–2 green chilies, seeded and sliced

½ teaspoon salt

½ teaspoon ground black pepper

2 tablespoons vegetable or olive oil

½ teaspoon ground turmeric

1 teaspoon ground cumin

1 teaspoon ground coriander

10–12 black olives, pitted

10–12 capers

8–10 fresh basil leaves

1–2 teaspoons chopped fresh cilantro

FOR THE DRESSING

½ cup natural yogurt

2 tablespoons honey

2 tablespoons tomato paste

1 tablespoon vegetable oil

½ teaspoon garlic pulp

½ teaspoon ginger pulp

salt

There are some days when I don't want to eat any meat or fish and it is then that I find this dish satisfying and nutritionally healthy. It is a versatile recipe to which you can add any favorite vegetables or eliminate anything you do not like. This is my "personal" version. It makes a good accompaniment to Blackened Spiced Cod (see page 83), or serve it simply with naan bread and poppadums.

Heat the oven to 350–400°F.

Put all the ingredients for the dressing into a blender, add salt to your taste, and blend to a smooth paste; set aside until the vegetables are ready.

Spread the vegetables evenly on a cookie sheet. Mix together the salt, pepper, oil, ground turmeric, ground cumin, and ground coriander and stir into the vegetables with a wooden spoon. Sprinkle with the olives, capers, basil leaves, and fresh cilantro.

Cook the vegetables under a heated broiler for 10–12 minutes. Turn off the broiler and place the vegetables in the oven for 5–7 minutes.

Serve hot, drizzled with the prepared dressing.

BLACKENED SPICED COD

serves four

1 tablespoon fennel seeds

1 teaspoon mustard seeds

1 teaspoon cumin seeds

1-inch piece cinnamon stick

1 teaspoon ground turmeric

½ teaspoon ground black pepper

1 teaspoon ginger pulp

1 teaspoon salt

4 x 5–6 ounce thick cod fillets,
    skin on

2 tablespoons vegetable oil

FOR THE SAUCE

1 teaspoon butter

3 tablespoons orange juice

1 tablespoon chopped fresh cilantro

1 green chili, finely chopped (optional)

This dish is a specialty from Mumbai (formerly Bombay), the city where I was born. Cod is my favorite fish for this recipe, but you can also use sea bass, haddock, or even skate. Serve it hot with a plain green salad or Tandoori Broiled Vegetables (see page 81) and poppadums.

Put the fennel seeds, mustard seeds, cumin seeds and cinnamon in a coffee grinder and blend to a fine powder. Mix the ground turmeric, black pepper, ginger, and salt into this mixture.

Dust each fish fillet with this blend of spices. Heat the oil in a nonstick skillet and sear the fish for 2-3 minutes on each side. Place in a serving dish and set aside.

Make the sauce by melting the butter in a pan with the remaining ingredients. Bring to a boil, then pour over the fish and serve while still hot.

INDIAN FRIED FISH

serves four

1 teaspoon ground turmeric

¾ teaspoon cayenne pepper

2 teaspoons ginger pulp

1 teaspoon lemon juice

1 teaspoon ground coriander

1 teaspoon ground cumin

1 teaspoon salt

½ teaspoon asafoetida (optional)

4 x 5–6 ounce cod or haddock fillets

FOR THE COATING

4 tablespoons chickpea flour (besan)

1 tablespoon rice flour

¾ teaspoon salt

½ teaspoon ground turmeric

1 teaspoon garam masala

vegetable oil, for frying

1 egg, beaten

In India, something as simple as fried fish can be made exotic, as this recipe demonstrates. Serve it hot with plain rice, Gujarati Dal (see page 95), and lime pickle, or have it as a snack you can eat with your fingers.

Combine the ground turmeric, cayenne, ginger, lemon juice, ground coriander, ground cumin, salt, and asafoetida together in a small bowl.

Dry the fish on paper towels and smear both sides of each piece with the blended spice mixture; set aside for 15 minutes so the flavors have time to penetrate.

Meanwhile, combine all the dry ingredients for the coating, and pour the oil for frying into a shallow skillet—enough to cover the bottom of the pan.

Heat the oil. Take each fish fillet, dip it into the beaten egg and then coat with the spiced flour. When the oil is hot, shallow fry each piece of fish for 3 minutes on one side. Turn over and fry for 2 minutes longer.

Drain on paper towels, before serving hot.

home comforts

SPICED CHICKEN IN A TOMATO AND MINT SAUCE

serves four

4 skinned chicken breasts halves

⅔ cup natural yogurt

1 tablespoon ground coriander

1 tablespoon ground cumin

½ teaspoon ground turmeric

½ teaspoon salt

1 teaspoon very finely chopped green chili

6 tablespoons fresh bread crumbs

5 tablespoons vegetable oil or butter

FOR THE SAUCE

2 tablespoons vegetable oil

1 onion, finely chopped

3 cloves garlic, finely chopped

1 can (14-oz.) crushed tomatoes

2 tablespoons finely chopped mint leaves

1 tablespoon garam masala

¾ teaspoon ground turmeric

1 teaspoon cayenne pepper or dried chili
   flakes

1 teaspoon sugar

1 teaspoon salt

TO SERVE

Coriander and Mint Raita (see page 13)

naan bread

When my children have friends around I sometimes make this chicken without the sauce and serve it as a spicy chicken burger, with a mango chutney and mayonnaise spread.

Heat the oven to 350°F.

Flatten the chicken breasts with a mallet or rolling pin.

Mix together the yogurt, ground coriander, ground cumin, ground turmeric, salt, and green chili. Marinate the chicken in this mixture for 20–25 minutes at room temperature.

Tip the bread crumbs onto a shallow plate. Lift each chicken breast out of the marinade and gently coat with the bread crumbs. Heat the vegetable oil or butter in a pan and slowly shallow-fry the coated chicken, 2 at a time, for 5–7 minutes on each side over medium heat. Remove from the skillet and place on a greased cookie sheet. Bake the chicken in the oven for 15 minutes, or until completely cooked through.

Meanwhile, in another shallow pan, heat the oil for the sauce. Fry the onion and garlic until golden brown. Add the canned tomatoes, mint leaves, garam masala, ground turmeric, cayenne or dried chili flakes, sugar, and salt. Cover and simmer for 10 minutes.

Transfer the cooked chicken into the sauce, cover, and cook for 5 minutes longer. Drizzle with a little raita and serve hot with naan bread.

CHICKEN WITH
SCALLIONS

2 tablespoons vegetable oil

1 teaspoon cumin seeds

1 onion, chopped

1 teaspoon garlic pulp

½ teaspoon ground turmeric

2 teaspoons ground coriander

½ teaspoon cayenne pepper

1¾ cups chopped tomatoes

½ cup scallions chopped

12 ounces boneless chicken, cut into
   1–1½-inch cubes

1 teaspoon fennel seeds

1 teaspoon coriander seeds

½ teaspoon ground black pepper

½ teaspoon crushed red chilies

¼ cup light cream

½ teaspoon dried fenugreek leaves

1 tablespoon chopped fresh cilantro

1 teaspoon sugar

salt

chopped scallion greens, to garnish

My family love onions and this recipe reflects their passion, I like to cook this when we're all spending an evening at home together.

Heat the oil in a pan and add the cumin seeds. When they begin to crackle, add the chopped onion and fry for 10–15 minutes over medium heat.

Add the garlic pulp, ground turmeric, ground coriander, and cayenne. Fry for 1 minute, then add the chopped tomatoes. Continue to cook for 5–10 minutes before adding the scallion and chicken pieces. Cook over medium heat for 15 minutes, stirring occasionally.

In another pan, dry-fry the fennel seeds, coriander seeds, black pepper, and red chilies for 5–8 minutes, then crush using a mortar and pestle.

Add the crushed spice mix to the sauce together with the cream, fenugreek leaves, and chopped fresh cilantro. Add the sugar and salt to taste.

Serve hot, garnished with chopped scallion greens.

SLOW-COOKED CHICKEN
WITH **BABY ONIONS**

serves four

3 tablespoons vegetable oil

10–12 baby onions or shallots, peeled

2 green chilies, slit

8–10 curry leaves

2 onions, chopped

3 cloves garlic, crushed

1 teaspoon ginger pulp

2 teaspoons ground coriander

1 teaspoon cayenne pepper

½ teaspoon paprika

1¼ cups water or chicken stock

1 teaspoon salt

2¼ pounds skinned chicken thighs or
  drumsticks

½ teaspoon sugar

TO GARNISH

1 teaspoon chopped fresh mint

1 tablespoon chopped fresh cilantro

1 tomato, chopped

The Indian name for this dish, pyaz aur murgh ki haandi, tells you that it was traditionally made in an earthenware pot (haandi). If you don't have one you can use a slow cooker, crockpot, Dutch oven, or casserole, or in a saucepan.

Heat the oil in a large, flameproof casserole or in a saucepan. Sauté the baby onions or shallots gently for 2–3 minutes. Remove from the pan and place on paper towels.

Using the same oil, fry the chilies, curry leaves, and chopped onions for 5 minutes, or until the onions are light brown in color and slightly translucent. Add the garlic, ginger, ground coriander, cayenne, paprika, water or chicken stock, and salt. Bring to a boil and add the chicken. Reduce the heat and cook, uncovered, for 20–30 minutes.

Return the sautéed baby onions to the pan, together with the sugar, stir, and cook for 3–4 minutes longer.

Garnish with the mint, fresh cilantro leaves, and chopped tomato and serve hot with chapattis or naan bread.

RICE WITH GROUND LAMB

¾ cup basmati rice

¼ cup vegetable oil

2 cloves

2 green cardamom pods

2 x 1-inch pieces cinnamon stick

½ teaspoon cumin seeds

1 onion, chopped

1 tablespoon garlic pulp

1½ cups chopped tomatoes

1 teaspoon ground turmeric

½ teaspoon cayenne pepper

4 teaspoons ground coriander

2 teaspoons garam masala

9 ounces ground lamb

2 green chilies, slit

1 cup peeled and diced potatoes

1 tablespoon chopped fresh mint

1 tablespoon chopped fresh cilantro

salt

FOR THE DOUGH (TO SEAL THE VESSEL)

all-purpose flour, as required

water, as required

The Indian name for this recipe is dum kheema pulav, which translates as "rice cooked with ground lamb in a sealed vessel." A traditional ground recipe from the northwest of India, it is not as difficult to make as it sounds. Serve it hot with a fresh yogurt raita. For me, this is comfort food at its best—a one-pot dish that is perfect for cold wintry nights.

Heat the oven to 400°F.

Wash the rice in several changes of water then leave to soak for 10 minutes before draining well.

Heat the oil in a flameproof pan that has a lid and add the cloves, cardamom pods, cinnamon, and cumin seeds. When they begin to crackle add the chopped onions and fry over medium heat for 5-10 minutes.

Add the garlic pulp, chopped tomatoes, and the ground spices and stir well. Stir in the ground lamb and green chilies and continue to cook. After about 5 minutes, add the drained soaked rice, potatoes, and fresh herbs and mix well.

Add enough hot water to cover the rice plus a little extra— approximately $1/2$ inch over the level of rice; add salt to taste. Bring to a boil, then remove from the heat.

Make a thick dough using just flour and water. Roll out into a long sausage-shape strip and use it to seal the space between the pan and its lid to prevent any air getting into the pan.

Place the pan in the oven and cook for 30–45 minutes. Remove the dough and lid and serve the lamb hot.

LAMB IN A CASHEW NUT AND MINT SAUCE

⅔ cup cashew nuts

2 tablespoons vegetable oil

2 cloves

2 green cardamom pods

2 bay leaves

½ teaspoon cumin seeds

1 large onion, chopped

1½ teaspoons garlic pulp

1 teaspoon ginger pulp

1 cup chopped tomatoes

2 teaspoons ground coriander

½ teaspoon ground turmeric

12 ounces boneless lamb, cut into
    1–1½-inch cubes

1 tablespoon light cream

2 tablespoons chopped mint, plus a few
    extra leaves to garnish

1 tablespoon chopped fresh cilantro

1 teaspoon sugar

salt

This dish came about by accident when I was defrosting the refrigerator one day and had to use up the contents for the evening meal. Now I make it by popular demand.

Soak the cashew nuts in hot water for 2–3 hours, drain, and then work in a blender to a fine paste; set aside.

Heat the oil in a pan and add the cloves, cardamom pods, bay leaves, and cumin seeds. When they begin to crackle, add the chopped onions and fry over medium heat for 8–10 minutes.

Add the garlic pulp, ginger pulp, chopped tomatoes, ground coriander, and ground turmeric. Cook, stirring constantly, for another 5 minutes.

Stir the cashew-nut paste into the mixture and continue to cook for 5 minutes longer.

Add the diced lamb. Reduce the heat and leave to cook, covered, for 30 minutes.

Stir in the light cream, chopped mint, cilantro, and sugar and adjust the seasoning to taste. Serve hot, garnished with a few mint leaves and accompanied by some plain basmati rice (see page 12).

DRY SPICED CABBAGE

serves four

1½ tablespoons vegetable oil

½ teaspoon mustard seeds

½ teaspoon cumin seeds

¼ teaspoon asafoetida

½ teaspoon ground turmeric

5–6 curry leaves

1½ teaspoons ginger pulp

1 green chili, chopped

1 dried red chili

3¾ cups shredded cabbage

½ cup grated carrots

1 teaspoon sugar

salt

juice of ½ lemon

1 tablespoon chopped fresh cilantro

My daughter adores this vegetable dish—she always requests it when she is feeling under the weather! The lemon juice and fresh cilantro give it a lovely fresh taste.

Heat the oil in a pan and add the mustard seeds and cumin seeds. When they begin to crackle, add the asafoetida, ground turmeric, curry leaves, ginger, and chilies. Stir in the shredded cabbage and carrots.

Reduce the heat, cover the pan, and leave to cook for 15–20 minutes. Add the sugar and salt to taste. Sprinkle with lemon juice and chopped cilantro and serve hot or cold.

OKRA IN YOGURT

serves four

1 cup water

1½ cups full-fat natural yogurt

1¼ cups sugar

1½ teaspoons ginger pulp

1 green chili, chopped

1 tablespoon chickpea flour (besan)

pinch of salt

2 tablespoons vegetable oil, plus extra for
   deep-frying

15 okra, sliced into circles

½ teaspoon cumin seeds

½ teaspoon mustard seeds

pinch of asafoetida

6 curry leaves

chopped fresh cilantro, to garnish

This Gujarati okra dish is a great accompaniment to Kitcheri (see page 95).

Mix the water and yogurt together in a bowl. Stir in the sugar, ginger, green chili, chickpea flour, and a pinch of salt and keep whisking until the chickpea flour blends into the yogurt.

Heat the oil for deep-frying in a large heavy-bottomed pan to 350°F. Add the okra and fry for 5–8 minutes.

In another pan, heat the 2 tablespoons oil and add the cumin seeds, mustard seeds, asafoetida, and curry leaves. When the mustard seeds begin to crackle, reduce the heat and pour the yogurt mixture into the pan. Cook for 10–15 minutes until the yogurt begins to boil.

Add the deep-fried okra to the sauce, sprinkle with chopped fresh cilantro and serve.

Opposite: **Dry spiced cabbage**

KITCHERI

serves four

2 cups basmati rice

1½ cups red lentils

1½ cups green split lentils

2 teaspoons vegetable oil

4 cloves

1 teaspoon cumin seeds

1–2 green chilies, chopped

4–5 bay leaves

2–3 garlic cloves, finely chopped

1 onion, sliced

1 large carrot, diced or sliced

⅔ cup frozen peas, thawed

1 quart hot water

2 teaspoons salt

1 teaspoon ground turmeric

1 tablespoon cracked black pepper

1 tablespoon butter

This is a great winter dish, especially when your spirits are low and you don't want to cook an elaborate meal. It is an all-time favorite with my family! The texture of kitcheri is very like stodgy oatmeal, and it is best served with a spicy salad, Okra in Yogurt (see page 92) or natural yogurt and poppadums.

Mix the rice and lentils together in a large pan or bowl and rinse in several changes of water; drain well.

Heat the vegetable oil in a large pan and add the cloves and cumin seeds. When the cumin seeds begin to crackle and the cloves begin to swell, add the green chilies and bay leaves, followed immediately by the garlic, onion, carrot, green peas, washed lentils and rice mixture, hot water, salt, ground turmeric, black pepper, and butter.

Reduce the heat and cook until the rice and lentils are cooked, 20–25 minutes.

GUJARATI DAL

serves four

1¼ cups yellow lentils

1 teaspoon ground turmeric

1½ teaspoons jaggery or brown sugar

1 tablespoon vegetable oil

2 cloves

2 green cardamom pods

½ teaspoon cumin seeds

½ teaspoon mustard seeds

2 bay leaves

½ teaspoon asafoetida

juice of ½ lemon

chopped fresh cilantro, to garnish

Opposite: **Gujarati dal**

This is one of my favorites—a good dal can really revive the spirits!

Wash the yellow lentils in several changes of water. Put them in a pan with 4 times their quantity of water. Add the ground turmeric and boil for 30 minutes until the lentils are mushy.

Add the jaggery or brown sugar and a little salt to taste.

In another pan, heat the oil and add the cloves, cardamom pods, cumin seeds, mustard seeds, bay leaves, and asafoetida, then reduce the heat. When the seeds begin to crackle, pour the mixture over the cooked lentils and stir well.

Stir in the lemon juice and sprinkle with chopped fresh cilantro to garnish.

GOAN RICE

2½ cups basmati rice

1 tablespoon ghee or salted butter

1 tablespoon cumin seeds

1 large onion, sliced

2–4 bay leaves

8–10 cloves

2-inch piece cinnamon stick

8–10 whole peppercorns

8–10 green cardamom pods, slightly opened

3½ cups boiling water

2 tablespoons shredded coconut

1½ teaspoons salt

½ teaspoon ground turmeric

1 tablespoon roasted cashew nuts, chopped

This rice recipe is famous along the western coast of India. It combines a variety of whole spices and is served with both vegetarian and non-vegetarian dishes. The spices will not cause any harm if eaten, but they might be too strong for some tastes. Alternatively, the whole spices can easily be removed from the rice after cooking.

Wash the rice in several changes of water, then leave to soak for 10 minutes before draining well.

Melt the ghee or butter in a pan and add the cumin seeds. When they begin to crackle, add the sliced onion and fry until light golden brown. Add the rest of the whole spices and sauté for 1–2 minutes longer over medium heat.

Reduce the heat and add the drained soaked rice. Using a wooden spoon, fold and turn the rice grains gently until all the grains are moistened and coated with the ghee and spiced onion mixture. The grains will start to gradually separate. At this point add the boiling water, coconut, salt, and ground turmeric.

Return to the boil. Partially cover the pan and cook for 15 minutes over medium heat.

Add the cashew nuts, re-cover the pan, reduce the heat, and cook for 5 minutes longer: the water should all be absorbed. Turn off the heat, stir the rice with a wooden spoon, and serve hot.

Tip You can easily replace the shredded coconut with 7 tablespoons canned coconut milk, if preferred. Just use 2½ cups boiling water instead of 3½ cups.

FRIED **SWEET POTATOES**

serves four

4 sweet potatoes

1 tablespoon ghee or butter

3 teaspoons sugar

4 scoops vanilla ice cream

½ teaspoon ground cinnamon

This traditional farmers' dessert is easy to make, affordable, and delectable. I love to eat this with vanilla ice cream.

Boil the whole sweet potatoes in their skins for 10–15 minutes or until tender; peel and cut into dice.

Melt the ghee or butter in a pan. Add the sugar and reduce the heat. When the sugar begins to caramelize, add the diced sweet potatoes and mix well.

Divide the sweet potatoes among 4 serving dishes and serve hot with a scoop of vanilla ice cream sprinkled with ground cinnamon.

COCONUT CREPES

FOR THE CREPES

scant 1 cup all-purpose flour

1 egg

pinch of salt

1¼ cups milk

1 tablespoon butter, melted

FOR THE FILLING

1 cup grated fresh coconut

1 tablespoon sugar

pinch of ground nutmeg or ground
    cardamom or drop of vanilla extract

TO SERVE

honey or maple syrup

vanilla ice cream

Surprise the family with this recipe the next time they ask for sweet crepes!

To make the crepe batter, mix the flour, egg, and salt together in a bowl. Pour the milk in slowly and whisk to form a thin batter, making sure there are not any lumps. Add a little water to thin down if necessary and finally stir in the melted butter.

Heat a nonstick 5-inch crepe pan. Pour in a little of the batter, about 3 tablespoons, tilting the pan slightly to cover the bottom completely with the crepe mixture; cook for about 2 minutes. Turn the crepe over and cook the other side for 2 minutes longer. Remove from the pan and keep warm while you make another 7 crepes in the same way.

Mix all the crepe filling ingredients together in a bowl. Place each crepe on a plate, one at a time. Spread a spoonful of the mixture down the middle of the pancake and roll up.

Serve the pancakes with either honey or maple syrup and a scoop of vanilla ice cream.

CHAI

serves four

4 teaspoons tea leaves

2¼ cups water

1 cup skim or whole milk

4–6 teaspoons sugar (optional)

¼ teaspoon green cardamom pods,
    coarsely crushed in a coffee grinder

½ teaspoon ginger pulp

1-inch piece cinnamon stick

2–3 cloves garlic, coarsely crushed

6–7 mint leaves

This spiced tea is served in India every time you ask for tea. In India tea is never served by itself, but usually accompanied by fried onion bhajis, Bombay mix, or toasted sandwiches.

I have often been asked for this recipe, which I prepare at home every morning. Instead of tea bags I use loose Darjeeling tea leaves, which is messy, but worth the effort. Omit the milk if you prefer your tea "black" but replace it with the same quantity of water.

Combine all the ingredients in a large saucepan. Bring to a boil then reduce the heat and simmer for 2–3 minutes.

Turn off the heat. Cover and leave to rest for 1 minute.

Strain and serve while still hot.

Opposite: **Coconut pancakes**

A special occasion means so many different things to different people—for some, Christmas is the ultimate special day, while everyone has different ways of celebrating birthdays and anniversaries. In India, there are hundreds of reasons to celebrate, from major religious feast days to harvest celebrations—Diwali, the Festival of Lights, is the most widely celebrated festival. I've included some really special dishes in this chapter, from rich meat dishes to saffron-scented desserts and sweets.

special
occasions

LETTUCE ROLLS

16 iceberg lettuce leaves

1 tablespoon butter

½ teaspoon whole cumin seeds

4 tablespoons chopped red bell pepper

1 cup finely chopped mushrooms

1 small onion, finely chopped

1 small carrot, grated

1–2 green chilies, finely chopped

½ teaspoon ground coriander

½ teaspoon salt

½ teaspoon asafoetida (optional)

2 tablespoons grated cheddar cheese

natural yogurt, Cilantro and Mint Raita
  (see page 13), or sweet mango chutney,
  to serve

This is a great vegetarian appetizer and is quite a recent innovation in Indian cooking.

Cut each lettuce leaf into a 3 x 6-inch rectangle.

Melt the butter in a shallow skillet and add the cumin seeds. When they begin to crackle, add all the vegetables and spices and cook over medium heat for 5 minutes. Turn off the heat, sprinkle with the grated cheese, and leave to cool.

Blanch the lettuce leaves in boiling water for 45 seconds. Dip them in iced water, drain, and pat dry with paper towels.

Divide the cooled vegetable filling mixture into 16 portions and put each portion on a flat lettuce leaf. Fold one long edge of each leaf rectangle toward the middle and then roll up from one short edge to make small "wraps."

Serve the lettuce rolls at room temperature with natural yogurt, Cilantro and Mint Raita or sweet mango chutney.

HOT CHILI SORBET

1¾ seeded and chopped green bell
  peppers,

4–6 green chilies, seeded and chopped

1 cup water

2 tablespoons chopped fresh mint

6 teaspoons sugar

½ teaspoon salt

TO GARNISH

unpeeled cucumber slices

sliced red bell pepper

sliced red chilies

Delight guests by serving this unique dish between courses.

Place the bell peppers and chilies in a food processor or blender, add the water, and work into a puree.

Transfer the puree to a pan. Add the mint, sugar, and salt and bring to a boil. Turn off the heat and leave to cool.

Press the cooled puree mixture through a strainer, pressing hard to push all the puree through the mesh. Pour into small molds or ice-cube trays and freeze for about 1 hour.

To serve, dip the bottom of the molds into hot water to ease removal of the sorbet. Turn the sorbet out onto individual serving dishes, arranging a slice of cucumber surrounded by long thin slivers of red pepper and chili on top of each.

GINGERED CRAB

serves four

4 medium to large uncooked crabs

2 tablespoons vegetable oil

2 teaspoons coriander seeds

3 onions, chopped

3 teaspoons ginger pulp

3 cloves garlic, crushed

3 green or fresh red chilies, chopped

3 bay leaves

3 teaspoons poppy seeds

2 tablespoons chopped fresh cilantro

11 ounces canned crushed tomatoes

1¼ cups canned coconut milk

1 tablespoon garam masala

1½ teaspoons salt

3 tablespoons ground cashew nuts
   (optional)

This is a popular dish from Mumbai, where it is known as adraki kekda. You can use either fresh or frozen crabs—I usually go to the fish market and pick the "fleshy" or "meaty" ones. Indian crabs are a grayish-black in color. Serve hot with rice, poppadums, and a raita.

If you are using live crabs, blanch them in boiling water for 2 minutes, then leave to cool. Remove all the meat from the shells.

Heat the oil in a deep skillet and add the coriander seeds. When they begin to crackle and lightly brown, add the onions, ginger, garlic, chilies, and bay leaves.

Cook for 5–8 minutes over medium heat before adding the poppy seeds, half the chopped fresh cilantro, and the tomatoes. Continue cooking for 10 minutes, then add the coconut milk, half the garam masala, the salt, and the cashew nuts, if using. Cook, uncovered, for 5 minutes longer.

Put the crab flesh in the sauce and cover the pan. Reduce the heat and bring to a simmer. Cook for 25 minutes, or until the crab meat is cooked through and flakes easily.

Sprinkle with the remaining chopped cilantro and garam masala. Turn off the heat, cover, and let stand for 5 minutes before serving.

Tip The sauce can be made 3 or 4 days in advance and kept in the refrigerator. Reheat it thoroughly before adding the crabmeat.

SHRIMP BALICHOW

serves four

6–8 cloves

1-inch cinnamon stick

1½ teaspoons black mustard seeds

4 tablespoons vegetable oil

2¼ pounds raw large shrimp (thawed
weight, if frozen), shelled and deveined

2 large onions, chopped

2 large tomatoes, chopped

1 cup malt vinegar

2 teaspoons ginger pulp

4 teaspoons garlic pulp

1½ teaspoons ground cumin

6–8 chopped hot red chilies

2 tablespoons brown sugar

1½ teaspoons salt

*Originally called shrimp balcho, this was a main dish that has
now become a relish or pickle, best served with flaky parathas
(see page 12).*

Grind the cloves, cinnamon, and mustard seeds coarsely in a
coffee grinder.

Heat the oil in a pan and fry the shrimp for 2–3 minutes.
Remove the shrimp from the oil, using a slotted spoon, and
leave to drain on paper towels. Cook the onions in the same oil
until translucent, 5–8 minutes.

Add the tomatoes and cook for 8–10 minutes. Add the
vinegar, ginger, garlic, ground cumin, red chilies, and the
ground cloves mixture. Stir and cook, uncovered, for
10 minutes.

Return the fried shrimp to the pan, together with the sugar
and salt. Cook for 5–8 minutes until the sauce reduces to a
thick gravy consistency.

SCALLOPS COOKED WITH
MILD GOAN SPICES

serves four

4 teaspoons butter

3 shallots or small red onions, finely diced

2 x 1-inch pieces cinnamon stick

6 cloves

5 scallions, finely chopped

1 fresh green chilli, finely diced (optional)

7 tablespoons dry white wine

½ teaspoon salt

½ teaspoon freshly cracked black pepper

1 tablespoon heavy cream

1½ pounds scallops

scant 1 cup water

2 teaspoons lemon juice

pinch of ground nutmeg

1 teaspoon chopped fresh cilantro
   (optional)

The state of Goa on the west coast of India is famous for its seafood dishes. I first ate this delicately spiced dish from the northern beach huts in Goa, and it has now become a firm favorite when I am cooking for a special occasion.

Melt the butter in a pan and cook the shallots or red onions for 3–4 minutes. Add the cinnamon, cloves, scallions, and chili. Add the wine, cover, and cook for 10–12 minutes. Add the salt, pepper, and cream.

Place the scallops in a separate pan and add the water and lemon juice. Simmer slowly for 10 minutes. Pour the spiced onion and wine sauce, which should be fairly thick, onto a plate and add the drained scallops. Season to taste. Sprinkle with ground nutmeg and chopped fresh cilantro, if using, and serve.

SOUR FISH CURRY

serves four

2¼ pounds cod or pomfret, thinly sliced

1 teaspoon ground turmeric

1 teaspoon salt

1 tablespoon coriander seeds

1 tablespoon cumin seeds

6 dried red chilies

6 cloves

1-inch piece cinnamon stick

2 tablespoons vegetable oil

2 onions, finely chopped

4 tablespoons shredded coconut

1 tablespoon ginger pulp

1 tablespoon garlic pulp

1 tablespoon vinegar

1¼ cups water

2 tablespoons tamarind pulp

A Goan dish, this curry was originally introduced by the Portuguese to India with fewer spices than today's typical recipe. Serve the curry hot with plain steamed or boiled rice.

Marinate the fish slices by rubbing ground turmeric and salt over them; set aside for 20 minutes.

Dry-fry the coriander and cumin seeds, dried red chilies, cloves, and cinnamon in a skillet for 2–3 minutes. Put the spices in a coffee grinder and grind to a coarse blend.

Heat the oil in a pan. Add the onions and fry until golden brown. Add the shredded coconut, ground spice blend, ginger, and garlic to the pan and cook for 2 minutes, or until the coconut begins to brown.

Add the vinegar and the water and bring to a boil. Lower the fish slices into the sauce and simmer for 5–7 minutes.

Stir in the tamarind pulp. Adjust the seasoning to taste and serve hot.

CHICKEN WITH SPINACH AND FENUGREEK

serves four

1½ tablespoons vegetable oil

1⅓ cups chopped tomatoes

7 tablespoons water

⅓ cup cashew nuts

1 teaspoon dried fenugreek leaves

1 teaspoon ground cardamom

1½ teaspoons sugar

salt

12 ounces boneless chicken, cut into
   1–1½-inch cubes

1½ cups whole baby spinach leaves

6 tablespoons light cream

This dish uses spinach leaves, but watercress can also be used.

Place the oil, chopped tomatoes, water, and cashew nuts in a pan and cook over medium heat for 15-20 minutes. Blend in a food processor until a fine puree forms.

Return to the pan and reheat. Add the fenugreek leaves and ground cardamom, followed by the sugar and a little salt to taste. Stir in the chicken pieces and cook for 15 minutes over medium heat, stirring occasionally.

Add the spinach leaves and cook for 3–4 minutes. Stir in the cream and serve garnished with "streaks" of light cream.

Opposite: **Chicken with spinach and fenugreek**

CHICKEN IN CARDAMOM CREAM SAUCE

serves four

2 tablespoons vegetable oil

1 teaspoon cumin seeds

2 cloves

3 green cardamom pods

2 bay leaves

2 medium onions, chopped

2 teaspoons ground coriander

2 tomatoes, chopped

12 ounces boneless chicken, cut into
   1–1½-inch cubes

7 tablespoons light cream

2 teaspoons ground cardamom

½ teaspoon dried fenugreek leaves

1 teaspoon garam masala

½ teaspoon sugar

salt

Green cardamoms grow on small bushes, whose stems spread themselves on the ground from which the pods grow. Whenever I am in south India on a visit to the plantations in the famous Cardamom Hills, I like to get fresh cardamoms that haven't yet been dried for consumer use. This recipe, however, uses dried cardamoms, which is their most widely available form.

Heat the oil in a pan and add the cumin seeds, cloves, cardamom pods, and bay leaves. When they begin to crackle, add the chopped onions and fry for 5–10 minutes over medium heat.

Add the ground coriander and chopped tomatoes and fry for 2 minutes longer.

Add the diced chicken and fry, stirring continuously, for about 5 minutes.

Add the light cream, ground cardamom, fenugreek leaves, and garam masala. Bring to a boil and simmer for 10–15 minutes. Add the sugar and salt to taste. Serve hot.

Tip Instead of using ready ground cardamom, you might like to grind whole green cardamom pods yourself. Crush the pods with a mortar and pestle to crack the outer shells. The black seeds inside are the spice, so remove the cracked pods before grinding the seeds.

AROMATIC SPICED LAMB

serves four

This is an authentic Hyderabadi dish eaten at festive occasions.

2 tablespoons vegetable oil

½ teaspoon mustard oil

2 onions, sliced

1 tablespoon garlic pulp

1 teaspoon ginger pulp

1 teaspoon ground cardamom

1½ pounds boneless boned lamb, cut into
    (1–1½ inch) cubes

1 teaspoon ground coriander

1 teaspoon ground cumin

¼ teaspoon ground nutmeg

¼ teaspoon ground cinnamon

4 tablespoons natural yogurt

1 teaspoon ground black pepper

1½ teaspoons salt

1 teaspoon sliced fresh ginger root, to
    garnish

Heat the vegetable and mustard oils in a large, heavy-bottomed pan. Add the sliced onions and cook over medium heat for 10–15 minutes, or until the onions are dark brown.

Add the garlic, ginger, and ground cardamom. Cook, stirring, for 2–3 minutes. Add the lamb and all the other ingredients. Cover with a tight lid and cook until the lamb is tender—about 30 minutes: add a little water if the meat begins to stick to the pan.

Serve hot, garnished with sliced ginger.

LAMB IN A CREAMY SAUCE

serves four

⅔ cup cashew nuts

2 tablespoons vegetable oil

1 teaspoon cumin seeds

2 cloves

2 bay leaves

2 green cardamom pods

1 large onion, sliced

3 teaspoons garlic pulp

1 teaspoon ground turmeric

½ teaspoon cayenne pepper

1 teaspoon garam masala

2 teaspoons ground coriander

12 ounces boneless lamb, cut into
    1–1½-inch cubes

7 tablespoons light cream

salt

1 tablespoon chopped fresh cilantro, to
    garnish

This creamy lamb curry is cooked at festive occasions. The ground cashew nuts help give it a deliciously rich consistency. As an alternative garnish, sprinkle with toasted almond slivers.

Soak the cashew nuts in hot water for 2–3 hours, then drain and grind to a fine paste; set aside.

Heat the oil in a pan. Add the cumin seeds, cloves, bay leaves, and cardamom pods. When they begin to crackle, add the sliced onions and fry for 5–10 minutes over medium heat.

Add the garlic pulp, ground turmeric, cayenne, garam masala, and ground coriander. Sprinkle with a little water and continue to cook for 2–3 minutes.

Add the cubed lamb and fry for 5 minutes to seal the meat on all sides.

Add the cashew nut paste and mix well. Add a little water if the mixture becomes too thick and continue to cook for 20–25 minutes, covered, over low heat.

Remove the lid, add the light cream to the curry and add salt to taste. Cook, uncovered, for 5 minutes to dry off any excess moisture.

Serve garnished with fresh cilantro.

Tip Toasted almond slivers make an attractive garnish. Simply heat a cast-iron skillet until hot and add the almond slivers. Toss the almonds for a few minutes in the hot pan, making sure they do not burn.

SMOKED LAMB
WITH **SAFFRON**

serves four

4 tablespoons milk

8–10 saffron strands

1 tablespoon vegetable oil

1½ pounds boneless lamb, cut into
  1–1½-inch cubes

2 onions, chopped

2 cloves garlic, chopped

7 tablespoons water

½ teaspoon salt

2 teaspoons paprika

1 red bell pepper, cut into strips

2 tomatoes, diced

2–3 green chilies

Simple, easy, and delicious, this dish comes from the southern city of Hyderabad. I sometimes make it with chicken or pork instead of lamb. Serve it with cumin rice (see page 13) or naan bread.

Heat the milk and soak the saffron strands in the hot liquid.

Meanwhile, heat the oil in a pan and sear the meat until brown all over; remove the meat from the oil and set aside.

Fry the onions in the same oil until translucent. Add the garlic and fry for 1–2 minutes. Return the seared meat to the pan. Add the water, cover, and cook for 25–30 minutes, or until the lamb is tender.

Add the salt, paprika, red pepper, and diced tomatoes. Continue cooking, covered, for 5 minutes over medium heat.

Meanwhile, dry-fry the green chilies in a skillet until the outside skins start to blacken in spots. Reduce the heat and continue tossing the chilies in the pan until all the green skin turns blackish-brown. Remove the chilies from the pan and grind them in a coffee grinder, or coarsely crush or chop them.

Add the saffron and milk to the meat and bring to a boil; turn off the heat. Sprinkle the smoked chili onto the meat. Cover and leave to stand for 5 minutes before serving.

POTATOES AND GREEN BELL PEPPERS COOKED WITH PEANUTS AND COCONUT

serves four

2 tablespoons vegetable oil

½ teaspoon cumin seeds

1½ teaspoons ginger pulp

1 green chili, chopped

1 green bell pepper, seeded and diced

1½ cups diced boiled potatoes

½ cup crushed peanuts

1 teaspoon sugar

1 teaspoon ground cumin

juice of ½ lemon

salt

2 tablespoons shredded coconut or grated
  fresh coconut

2 tablespoons chopped fresh cilantro

This potato, peanut, and coconut dish is commonly eaten by the farmers of Maharashtra. I've given it a new twist by adding green bell peppers.

Heat the oil in a pan and add the cumin seeds. When they begin to crackle, add the ginger and green chili and reduce the heat. Add the diced green pepper and continue to fry over low heat.

After 2–3 minutes stir in the boiled potatoes, then the crushed peanuts. Add the sugar, ground cumin, lemon juice, and salt to taste and mix well.

Serve sprinkled with grated coconut and chopped fresh cilantro.

MINT AND
POTATO PULAV

serves four

1¼ cups basmati rice

3 tablespoons mint leaves, plus extra
   to garnish

3 cloves garlic

½-inch piece fresh ginger root

1 green chili

1 tablespoon chopped fresh cilantro

4 tablespoons vegetable oil

3 cloves

3 green cardamom pods

3 bay leaves

½ teaspoon cumin seeds

1 onion, chopped

2 potatoes, peeled and diced

salt

Mint is not the most commonly used herb in Indian dishes, but this fresh tasting mint and rice dish from the southern state of Hyderabad is wonderful served with a lamb curry like Smoked Lamb with Saffron (see page 112).

Wash the rice in several changes of water, then leave, to soak for 10 minutes before draining well.

Combine the mint leaves, garlic, ginger, chili, and fresh cilantro in a blender and work to a fine paste; add a little water if required.

Heat the oil in a pan, then add the cloves, cardamom pods, bay leaves, and cumin seeds. When they begin to crackle, add the chopped onion and fry over medium heat.

When the onions begin to soften, add the potatoes, drained soaked rice, and mint paste mixture; stir gently. Add enough hot water to come to a level ½-inch above the layer of rice. Add salt as required and bring to a boil.

Once the water begins to boil, reduce the heat to a simmer, cover with a lid, and leave to cook. After 15–20 minutes, remove the lid and check whether the rice is cooked. Stir once gently to avoid the rice breaking up. Replace the lid and turn off the heat.

After about 5 minutes transfer the pulav to a serving bowl. Serve hot, garnished with a few mint leaves, and with a fresh raita as an accompaniment (see pages 13–14).

SMOKED PUREED
EGGPLANTS WITH SPICES

serves four

3 large eggplants

2 tablespoons vegetable oil

½ teaspoon cumin seeds

1-inch piece fresh ginger root, chopped

1 green chili, chopped

1 large onion, chopped

2 teaspoons garlic pulp

½ teaspoon ground turmeric

½ teaspoon cayenne pepper

1 teaspoon ground coriander

1¾ cups chopped tomatoes

1 teaspoon ground cumin

salt

1 tablespoon chopped fresh cilantro, to
   garnish

I absolutely adore eggplants—they are one of my favorite vegetables, which is why I like to prepare this dish for special family occasions. It is great as an accompaniment, but sometimes I also combine it with yogurt and serve it as a dip with plain poppadums.

Heat the oven to 475°F.

Rub the skins of the eggplants with 1 tablespoon of the oil. Place them on a cookie sheet and cook in the oven for 15–20 minutes until the outer skin burns and the inner flesh is soft. Remove the skins when cool enough to handle and put the flesh in a bowl; set aside

Heat the remaining oil in a pan and add the cumin seeds. When they begin to crackle, add the chopped ginger and green chili. After 1 minute add the chopped onions and fry for 4–5 minutes.

Stir in the garlic pulp and continue to fry. Add the ground turmeric, cayenne, and ground coriander. Sprinkle with water and fry for a minute longer.

Add the chopped tomatoes and continue to cook over medium heat for 5–8 minutes.

Place the eggplant pulp on a chopping board and chop with a large knife, then stir into the spicy "masala." Add the ground cumin and salt to taste, sprinkle with chopped fresh cilantro and serve.

Tip For an alternative dip, replace the eggplant pulp with an equal quantity of mashed potatoes.

FENUGREEK-FLAVORED
DEEP-FRIED BREAD

serves four

3 ounces fresh fenugreek leaves

salt

1¾ cups wholewheat flour

½ teaspoon ground turmeric

½ teaspoon cumin seeds

1 teaspoon ground cumin

½ teaspoon cayenne pepper

1 tablespoon chopped fresh cilantro

1 tablespoon oil, plus extra for deep-frying

natural yogurt, to serve

This deep-fried bread, methi puri, comes from western Gujarat and is commonly eaten with natural yogurt. It uses fresh fenugreek leaves, which are available by the bunch in most Indian food stores. Pick the leaves from the stem and wash them before use. Freeze any leaves left after making this recipe by drying them well on paper towels and freezing them in an airtight container.

Chop the fenugreek leaves, sprinkle with salt, and rub in well. Leave for 5–10 minutes, then squeeze the fenugreek leaves to remove excess juices and put in a bowl.

Add the flour to the bowl, together with the ground turmeric, cumin seeds, ground cumin, cayenne, chopped fresh cilantro, and a little salt.

Sprinkle in enough water to make a stiff dough. Add 1 tablespoon of oil and knead well using your hands; set aside for 30 minutes.

Divide the dough into 16 equal pieces. Roll out each piece on a floured board into a flat circle with a 3–4 inch diameter.

Heat the oil for deep-frying in a deep pan to 350°F. Deep-fry each puri, one at a time, for 45–60 seconds until golden brown. Remove from the pan with a slotted spoon and drain on paper towels.

Serve immediately with natural yogurt.

SAFFRON-SEMOLINA PUDDING

serves four

1½ teaspoons ghee

10–15 raisins

10–15 cashew nuts, roughly chopped

¾ cup plus 1 tablespoon semolina

⅓ cup sugar

1¼ cups milk

pinch of saffron strands

almonds slivers, to decorate (optional)

Saffron is considered the world's most expensive spice: gifts of saffron are exchanged at Diwali, the Hindu Festival of Lights, and this is traditionally a dessert made on festive occasions. If, like me, however, you have a sweet tooth, you will find you don't need an excuse to prepare this delicious treat.

Melt the ghee in a pan and add the raisins and chopped cashew nuts. After about 2 minutes, add the semolina, reduce the heat and cook, stirring, for 2–3 minutes.

Add the sugar and mix well. Pour in the milk and add the saffron. Cook over low to medium heat, whisking well.

When the mixture begins to thicken and the semolina is cooked, remove the pan from the heat. Decorate with slivers of almonds, if liked, and serve hot.

SAFFRON-FLAVORED
THICK YOGURT

serves four

2¼ cups natural yogurt

½ cup sugar

pinch saffron strands

7 tablespoons milk

Better than fruit yogurt, this dessert is commonly made during the summer months in India to counteract the scorching summer heat.

Tip the yogurt onto a piece of cheesecloth. Bring together the 4 corners of the cloth, tie them into a knot and hang the cloth of yogurt over a bowl or the sink to let the excess water from the yogurt drain away; leave overnight.

The next day, tip the drained, thick yogurt into a bowl and whisk in the sugar until it dissolves.

Heat the saffron and milk together in a pan and cook over low heat for 10–15 minutes until the milk reduces and becomes dark yellow in color. Whisk the milk into the yogurt.

Pour the yogurt mixture into 4 serving dishes. Refrigerate when cool and serve chilled.

Opposite: **Saffron-semolina pudding**

NUTTY BARFI

serves four

⅔ cup coarsely ground cashew nuts,
    or chopped cashew nuts (very small
    pieces)

⅔ cup coarsely ground shelled pistachios

⅔ cup coarsely ground almonds

½ cup shredded coconut

2 teaspoons ground green cardamom

1 teaspoon ground nutmeg

1½ cups sugar

¾ cup water

8–10 saffron strands steeped in 1 teaspoon
    hot water

7 ounces ghee

scant ½ cup coarse semolina

1 cup chickpea flour (besan)

TO DECORATE (OPTIONAL)

slivers of pistachios

slivers of almonds

saffron strands

I usually grind the nuts for this recipe in a coffee grinder. This barfi keeps well at room temperature for seven days. In a warmer climate, keep it in the refrigerator and simply heat for 30 seconds in a microwave before serving.

Mix all the chopped nuts, shredded coconut, ground cardamom, and nutmeg, in a large bowl.

Combine the sugar and water in a pan and heat until the sugar melts. Reduce the heat and simmer for 5–8 minutes. Mix the saffron together with this syrup.

Meanwhile, melt the ghee in a wok. When it becomes very hot and melts, reduce the heat and add the semolina. Cook, stirring continuously. After 10 minutes, or when the semolina turns golden brown, add the chickpea flour. Cook for 5 minutes, stirring continuously. Stir this mixture into the nuts, mixing well with a wooden spoon, then stir in the sugar syrup.

Pour the mixture while hot into a baking tray; leave to cool. Decorate the barfi with slivers of pistachios, almonds, and strands of saffron, if liked. Cut into diamond shapes and serve.

PISTACHIO AND COCONUT BARFI

serves four

4 tablespoons melted ghee

1¼ cups canned coconut milk

5 ounces milk powder

1½ cups shredded coconut

4 tablespoons water

¾ cup superfine sugar

2 teaspoons ground cardamom

6 tablespoons shelled chopped green
   pistachios

½ teaspoon ground nutmeg

saffron stands, to decorate (optional)

Like the Nutty Barfi (opposite), this dessert is often made for special occasions and always during Diwali.

Lightly grease a 10–11-inches baking pan with 1 teaspoon of the ghee. Melt the remaining ghee in a saucepan. Add the coconut milk and stir in the milk powder, making sure there are not any lumps in the mixture. Add the shredded coconut, water, sugar, ground cardamom, pistachios, and nutmeg and mix well: the mixture should be fairly thick.

Reduce the heat and continue to cook, stirring, for 5–7 minutes. Remove from the heat and empty the contents of the pan into the baking pan. Spread out the mixture and flatten it evenly. Smooth the top, sprinkle a few strands of saffron over, if using, and refrigerate for 4–5 hours.

Cut the barfi into squares, arrange on a serving dish, and serve chilled or at room temperature.

GLOSSARY OF INGREDIENTS

The following herbs and spices are referred to in many of the recipes in this book. Some of them may be more familiar than others and the majority are easily found in large supermarkets. Others may need to be purchased from a specialist food store or Asian grocery store. Indian names are in brackets.

Ajowan (ajwain)

Ajowan seeds look very similar to cumin seeds and have a strong, distinctive flavor that resembles aniseed. The spice is used to add a zing to many fish and vegetable dishes, as well as some Indian breads. The seeds are often chewed on their own to alleviate stomach pains.

Asafoetida (hing)

Asafoetida has a very overpowering, almost unpleasant smell, which is calmed when it is fried in oil. Asafoetida is made from a dried gum resin that is ground to a yellowish powder. It is used in small quantities in cooking in many lentil and vegetable dishes.

Cardamom (elaichi)

Cardamom has a delicate, aromatic fragrance, which is used to flavor meat and vegetable dishes, as well as desserts and drinks. It is an essential ingredient in garam masala (see page 11). You will see brown cardamom pods as well as the pale green ones, but the green ones have a much finer flavor.

Chat masala

This spice mix, made with salt, pepper, cumin seeds, ground ginger, and dried mango, is available already prepared from Asian food stores.

Chilies, dried (lal mirch)

There are a confusing number of chili varieties, but the most commonly used dried chilies in Indian cooking are the small, red ones—they will add a fiery heat to any dish. They can be used whole, crushed, flaked, or in powdered form. Remove the seeds before using to lessen the heat, if you wish.

Chilies, fresh (hari mirch)

I generally use the long thin green chilies when fresh ones are called for, although they can vary in heat so use with caution. The seeds can be removed to make them less fiery. Always wash your hands after handling chilies.

Cilantro, fresh (hara dhaniya)

Fresh green cilantro is used as a herb and has a lovely fresh fragrance. It is used to make chutneys and dips and makes a wonderful garnish.

Cinnamon (dalchini)

The spice used in cooking is the dried inner bark of the cinnamon tree. It is one of the earliest known spices and is an essential ingredient of garam masala. It is used in its "stick" form as well as a ground spice, and its warm, sweet aroma enhances rice dishes, as well as meat dishes and desserts. In Ayurvedic medicine, it is used to alleviate headaches, colds, and rheumatic pains.

Cloves (long)

Cloves are the small, dried buds of the clove tree, which have a sweet aroma, but a bitter taste. They are used to flavor rice and savory dishes and are also used in spice mixtures, such as garam masala.

Coriander seeds (dhaniya)

The pungent, slightly sweet, citrus flavor of coriander seeds is used in vegetable, meat, fish, and poultry dishes. The seeds come from a leafy herb bearing lacy flowers—these seeds are dried and used extensively, whole or ground, as an aromatic spice in Indian cooking. The whole seeds are often dry-roasted and then coarsely crushed with other spices to make a spice mixture. The flavor of the ground spice is not as intense as that of whole seeds.

Cumin (jeera)

The distinctive aroma of cumin seeds is used to flavor rice and curries. Cumin seeds are the fruits of a small annual herb that grows throughout India. They are used dried and range in color from light, greenish brown to dark brown. They can be fried in hot oil to intensify their flavor or dry-roasted and then ground with other spices. Ground cumin is available from supermarkets, but it quickly loses its flavor. Another variety of cumin is black cumin (kala jeera), although black cumin is less aromatic and not as bitter in flavor.

Curry leaves (kari patta)

This aromatic herb is used to add flavor to many dishes, particularly in southern India, but it also has medicinal properties and can ease stomach pains. Despite its name, it does not taste of curry, and is actually related to the lemon family. Curry leaves are fried in hot oil which brings out their nutty flavor. I often freeze curry leaves: wash them and then leave to dry on dish towels. Then put them into a bag and place in the freezer.

Fennel seeds (saunf)

Dried fennel seeds are used throughout India, not only to add a sweet, aniseed flavor to a variety of dishes, but also as a mouth freshener. They are similar in appearance to cumin seeds although greener in color.

Fenugreek (methi)

Fenugreek is used to flavor a variety of dishes and is also used in bread making (see page 117). It is one of the most powerful and ancient spices, believed to aid digestion. Its leaves are used both fresh and dried and the dried seeds are commonly used in ground spice mixes. Dried fenugreek leaves are often referred to as kasoori methi.

Ghee

Ghee is clarified butter that can be used for deep-frying without burning—it has a delicious buttery taste, although vegetable oil can be substituted in most cases. You can buy it in all Indian grocers.

Ginger (adrak)

Ginger has a pungent, fresh aroma and has been prescribed for many ailments—a ginger infusion is great for a sore throat or cold, as well as travel sickness and nausea. It is the underground root or rhizome of a herbaceous plant grown throughout Asia. In its fresh state ginger is most often used as a pulp to add a distinctive flavor to a variety of dishes. Dried ginger is also available as a ground spice that can be used to flavor drinks, as well as savory and sweet dishes.

Mustard seeds (rai)

Mustard seeds are used to flavor a variety of dishes, particularly those from Bengal. Whole black mustard seeds are often thrown into hot oil or "popped" at the beginning of a recipe—this gives them a sweet, nutty taste that enhances vegetables, legumes, and fish dishes. There are three types of mustard seeds, of which brown and black are the most widely used in India.

Nutmeg (jaiphal)

Nutmeg has a warm, sweet flavor and is used in small quantities in desserts, often grated from a whole nutmeg. It is also used in some garam masala mixes. Nutmeg is believed to help overcome bronchitis and rheumatism.

Pepper (kalimiri)

Pepper is the most commonly used spice and is sometimes known as the King of Spices. It is the fruit of a perennial vine, which bears berries or peppercorns. The black, white, red, and green varieties all come from the same plant—the difference in color occurs in the way they are processed. Black pepper is made by drying green peppercorns in the sun, while white pepper is made when ripe berries are softened in water, hulled, and then dried.

Saffron (kesar)

Saffron is considered the most expensive spice in the world and is worth its weight in gold. It is actually made from the stigmas of the crocus flower, which are hand picked and dried in the sun. A gift of saffron is something very special and it is often exchanged at Diwali. Saffron, which is sold as strands and as a powder, is used in very small quantities to flavor both savory and sweet dishes, particularly for special occasions.

Tamarind (imli)

The tamarind tree is evergreen and bears long, crescent-shaped pods. Within these pods are the seeds, surrounded by a fleshy pulp. It is this pulp, with its fruity sweet-and-sour aroma, that is used in Indian cooking. According to Ayurvedic medicine, it is beneficial as a mild laxative, and tamarind water is often recommended to soothe a sore throat.

Turmeric (haldi)

Although used mainly for color, this spice imparts a subtle flavor and is also used extensively for its antiseptic and digestive properties. This bright yellow, bitter-tasting spice is sold ground, although the small roots are also available fresh or dried. Like ginger, it needs to be peeled and ground before using. If your hands become stained when preparing fresh turmeric, you can clean them by rubbing them with potato peelings.

ACKNOWLEDGMENTS

Special thanks go to:

Everyone at New Holland Publishing, in particular my editor, Clare Sayer, and Rosemary Wilkinson, for all their hard work and for making the idea for the book come to life; Julie Saunders, for typing all the recipes and generally making my very busy life less hectic; the designer, Roger Hammond; John Freeman who, once again, has produced stunning photographs; Sunil Menon for his skill in styling the recipes, even when India were playing in the Cricket World Cup!

Everyone at Patak's, in particular those who were involved in the location photography. A special mention goes to the team at Nexus.

And last but not least, thanks to my family and friends, without whom I would not have had the inspiration to write this book.

The publishers would also like to thank the following for providing props for the photography:

Abu Sandeep Gallery
55 Beauchamp Place
London SW3 1NY, England
Tel: + 44 (0) 20 7584 7713

Alessi
22 Brook Street
London W1K 5DF, England
Tel: + 44 (0) 20 7518 9091

Cargo Homeshops
Tottenham Court Road
London W1P 7PL, England
Tel: + 44 (0) 20 7580 2895

John Lewis plc
Oxford Street
London W1A 1EX, England
Tel: + 44 (0) 20 7629 7711

Kara Kara
2a Pond Place
London SW3 6QZ, England
Tel: + 44 (0) 20 7591 0891

Muji
Branches throughout the UK
Tel: + 44 (0) 20 7287 7323

Neelam Sarees
388-390 Romford Road
London E7, England
Tel: + 44 (0) 20 8472 2410

The Pier
200 Tottenham Court Road
London W1P 7PL, England
Tel: + 44 (0) 20 7436 9642

Thomas Goode
195 South Audley Street
London W1K 2BN, England
Tel: + 44 (0) 20 7499 2823

INDEX

The Patak's story

Meena Pathak is the Director of Product Development for Patak's, the authentic Indian food brand. Patak's grew from very modest beginnings, and is now the number one worldwide Indian food brand—a household name, used by professional chefs and home cooks across the world.

Patak's was founded in the late 1950s by Laxmishanker Pathak, Meena's father-in-law, following his arrival in England with his wife and children. Laxmishanker experienced great difficulty in finding employment and as a means to survive, he began making and selling Indian samosas and snacks from his home. They were well received and soon he had raised sufficient capital to buy his first small shop in North London. The business expanded with the introduction of other authentic Indian products, including pickles and chutneys, and orders flooded in.

Kirit Pathak joined the family business at the age of 17. Meena herself became involved in Patak's shortly after her marriage to Kirit in 1976 when Kirit discovered her creative cooking abilities. Having trained in food technology and hotel management with the prestigious Taj hotel group, Meena had plenty of experience to offer. After a particularly delicious meal she had cooked for the family one evening, Kirit asked her, "Can you get that into a jar?," and her career in recipe and product development took off from there.

Throughout the 70s and 80s, the business prospered under Kirit and Meena's guidance. The product portfolio was extended to include poppadums and other Indian accompaniments and, in addition to supplying the Indian restaurant trade with pastes and chutneys, Patak's began exporting its range across the world into mainstream grocery markets.

Meena believes that the key to a successful Indian dish is not just the distinctiveness of the recipe, but also the quality and freshness of the

herbs, spices, and ingredients used. Because of this, Kirit personally supervizes the importation of the key ingredients from India and around the world. The herbs and spices are then ground at the factory in a unique grinding system, which guarantees the ingredients are as fresh as possible. The spice blends that form the basis of every Patak's recipe are known only to the members of the Pathak family.

The company's range has extended over the years from pickles and chutneys, to pastes and cooking sauces in jars and cans, prepared meals, poppadums, Indian breads and now includes Indian snacks and frozen and chilled meals.

Patak's products are now widely available, enabling consumers to produce their favorite Indian meals at home.

For more information on the company, visit the web site at www.pataks.co.uk.